11/19/09
To Terry,
Keep on learning!
Fear Nothing.
You are in
my best thoughts.

BECOMING A STORYTELLER

WISDOM, TRAUMA AND THE DALAI LAMA

William Schmidt

WILLIAM SCHMIDT PH.D

authorHOUSE®

AuthorHouse™
1663 Liberty Drive
Bloomington, IN 47403
www.authorhouse.com
Phone: 1-800-839-8640

First published by AuthorHouse 10/6/2009

ISBN: 978-1-4389-8545-9 (sc)
ISBN: 978-1-4389-8546-6 (hc)

Printed in the United States of America
Bloomington, Indiana

This book is printed on acid-free paper.

To Ana Beatriz, my wife and best friend
and
to our children
Ana Leticia, John, and Bill

And

to my Jesuit friend Ignacio Martin-Baro
Whose example I follow

TABLE OF CONTENTS

INTRODUCTION

I leaned back into my wooden chair, listening to the energetic, middle-aged woman address the topic of relationships.

"Trauma," Pia Mellody stated, "is any experience that is non-nurturing."

It was an "a-ha" moment for me.

I have always believed that if one can tell a story about an experience, one can heal that experience. In fact, this is how I make my living. I am a mental health counselor. I listen to stories. I am fascinated by how people make sense of their lives and experiences. Can storytelling lead to wisdom and to healing?

Yes.

Trauma does not doom a person to a lifetime of sadness. On the contrary … think about the wisest, happiest person that you know. Do you have such a person in mind? Hasn't this person suffered trauma and moved through it? Trauma and all non-nurturing experiences can be the key to freedom and to happiness. All true healers have themselves shared their stories of trauma and through the process have found healing. Only the wounded can become wise.

Happiness is a by-product of healthy relationships. When trauma is identified and healed ("processed" in the language of therapy), a person is more capable of sustaining healthy relationships. However, if trauma lingers unresolved, unidentified, and unhealed, relationships are left unsatisfying, disappointing, and non-nurturing. Healthy relationships, characterized by appropriate, discerning boundaries, are more elusive when trauma goes unidentified and unhealed.

Those who have engaged in therapy know the experience of sitting with, surfacing, and sharing one's story. One's affective life, relationships, and behaviors often reflect a skewed, sometimes unsuccessful effort to deal with past trauma. I have written this book to help people share their stories. This is the first step on the healing journey.

There are people who have gone ahead of you that have faced difficulties similar to yours. How did Archbishop Oscar Romero deal with the misunderstandings of his church? How did Martin Luther King maintain hope in the face of economic injustice and institutional racism? How did Gandhi live and act non-violently when faced with violence and oppression? What message of hope and joy did Mother Theresa find amongst the "untouchable" and discarded? What message does the Prophet Mohammed offer you at a time when you feel fear?

These courageous witnesses have much to teach us. With a little research, and some imagination, one can reach across time and space to better understand trauma and adversity. In a therapeutic, healing exchange, every person can heal trauma, achieve wisdom, and live a fuller, more generous life.

I call this technique "dialogical journaling."

In dialogical journaling, one needs three things: a journal, a mentor, and a willingness to use one's imagination in a truthful fashion.

In the journal, one will write one's story. By applying ink to paper, experiences, sentiments, joys, and sorrows move from subjective, interior space into the objective world. The word *kenosis* is a Greek term meaning "emptying," and it is used by St. Paul in his letter to the Philippians. The apostle uses this term to describe Jesus' act of becoming human. The writing of one's own story forms a kind of *kenosis* in which one becomes more human and thus a greater manifestation of the divine. Secretive, often forgotten material that actively resides in the "shadow side" of one's unconscious or subconscious mind surfaces, or "empties out."

The body remembers what the mind chooses to forget. In the process of writing, one may come to see the meaning that is ascribed to one's experience, consciously or otherwise.

For those who have experienced trauma, it is in their interest, and the interest of others, to revisit these experiences. If not, unresolved trauma will invariably color the way one sees himself or herself and limit free, productive involvement in the surrounding world. Residual shame and guilt from life's experiences accumulate in the psyche. As one's experiences come into view through dialogical journaling, even the most painful experiences move towards resolution. In this process of naming experience, one moves towards becoming one's best self. One becomes more ready for healthy relationships. With a more positive attitude and deepened self-confidence, one is better equipped to engage with others in a more positive fashion.

Self-confident and extroverted people often find it easy to share their experiences with others. However, even extroverts experience shame and guilt post-trauma and are more likely to keep such experiences to themselves. They may try to "work it out" on their own terms. This strategy rarely resolves trauma. Pools of shame and guilt stagnate inside the deepest self. Trauma that is not resolved does not go away. The mind's ability to filter some experiences from consciousness is not limitless. The inability to let go of past events can lead to psychosomatic depression. Anxiety is a floating fear of an unknown and uncertain future. Both anxiety and depression are characteristic illnesses of time that represent an inability to live the present moment. With repressed or suppressed trauma, a past event subliminally replays itself. Such trauma silently colors perceptions and can lead to unhealthy relationships with people, places, and things. Trauma rests at the heart of codependency, compulsivity, and addiction.

As Dante explored the heights of heaven and probed the depths of hell, he always had a guide to accompany him on the journey. So, too, on this journey one might elect to choose an imaginary mentor as a wisdom figure for the journaling experience.

In whom does one place deep confidence and trust, such as a grandparent, a personal hero, a saint? It may be someone personally known and loved. It might be a figure from literature. Depending upon one's life experience, a historical figure might do the trick. The person may be living or dead. He or she may have had similar experiences or may have a different worldview. The principal quality of a mentor is integrity. He or she must be a person of truth and honesty. Identifying with this trusted other will enable growth towards one's best self.

The old adage, "what doesn't kill one will make one stronger" holds true. No experience is so terrible that one cannot learn from it and that one cannot grow through it. Hegelian philosophy proposed that reality comes into being through a series of dynamic, conflict-inducing encounters. "Thesis" collides headlong into "antithesis," through which a new "synthesis" results. Think again about the person you admire and consider wise. Did his or her wisdom come about through a reading of existing philosophical treatises? It likely came through his or her experience of struggle and the resolution of suffering.

T.S. Eliot wrote, "The last temptation is the greatest treason, to do the right thing for the wrong reason." Are there millionaires who have sought safety in wealth to mitigate feelings of loss and abandonment? Bulging bank accounts and walls boasting of achievements cannot heal feelings of betrayal and loss any better than marijuana or Johnny Walker. While wisdom is born of experience, each person must have the courage to reflect on that experience and so become rich in self-understanding. Each person's experience is unique, and the meaning one ascribes to that experience can be life-giving.

Books and theories can block an original insight into one's own experience. One must acknowledge one's own experience as it is and allow experience to speak directly to oneself. It is useless to dwell on an event as if by one's focus past history could be changed. Nor is it enough to store one's experience in one's psyche as if this were a warehouse for useless things. Like a miner panning for ore, one can bring the gold that is experience out into the light to discover its true meaning and value. One can invite one's mentor to hold the pan while one places the weight of one's experiences into his or her care. Together, one sifts through its contents. *In sterco,* believed the ancient alchemists, *invenitur.* "In the muck, the gold will be found."

The goal of all human life is transcendence. One is not the same today as yesterday. In every act, through every experience, one moves to some new stage of maturity, of uniqueness, of gift. Every human being manifests the divine. The name *Buddha* means the one who has awakened to this truth.

Can you become your best self in isolation? No. It is true that monks and hermits choose a solitary life in order to realize their best selves. Yet even in the eremitical experience, individuation results from a relationship to God and to community. Does joining a religious community enable a person to grow and mature into his or her best self? Most often, the answer is yes. A healthy religious community encourages its members to move beyond present levels of understanding to new insights, awareness, and levels of commitment. Healthy communities encourage their members to "keep moving" towards deepened self-understanding reflected in a commitment to doing justice, understood as "love in action." They avoid pre-fabricated, "one size fits all" solutions to life's questions and ends. An unhealthy religious community promotes conventionality and proclaims that virtue lies in adherence to the status quo. Pat answers may reduce one's internal stress. But simple solutions to life's questions may prevent one's growth and development. The paternalistic nature of organized religion can often make believers dependent upon those proposed as wiser. In unhealthy communities, power and access to truth may be restricted to the domain of ordained leadership.

When one supplies meaning to one's own experience, it can become messy. One may have joined a faith community because it forms a sort of shell that offers protection from the chaos and disorder of daily experience. Following one's own inner compass and living by hard-won, self-appropriated principles may seem heretical to some, but is a mark of sanctity to others.

As in Plato's metaphor of the cave, one must understand that to seek the truth of one's experience on honest terms, one may end up ejected from the community that one loves. In Plato's imagery, the philosopher, as a "lover of wisdom," ends up wandering throughout the world by himself or herself. Some people choose misery and sadness over joy and freedom because they fear disappointing the "community." They end up living lives marked by conformity and imagined security, wrapped in the mantle of self-sacrifice.

Self-censorship is akin to "writer's block." Dialogical journaling requires one to allow a free flow of ideas without permitting the "censor within" to edit the thoughts, memories, or experiences before they have the opportunity to see the light of day. This is the reason one must choose the mentor wisely. The main characteristic of the mentor is that he or she can be taken to have accomplished his or her own personal work. The mentor must have individuated and self-actualized. One's mentor must have "loved under fire." The mentor's life has made the world a better place. One definition of justice is "love in action." The journey towards individuation moves towards personal integration. To achieve this, one must be wholly and forthrightly honest about what one has experienced; one must be willing to name this experience "loud and clear." The mentor is there to help one to accomplish this journey.

One group of people which may help one in this process is the Twelve Step community. Beginning historically with Alcoholics

Anonymous, this movement has come to address a wide variety of issues: emotions, relationships, eating, love and sex addictions, gambling, etc.… In my mind, these groups are complementary and comprised of persons who, while admitting their brokenness, strive to transcend their present condition. Group members share their stories without imposing judgments in an atmosphere of anonymity and confidentiality. They experience the support of a community of men and women who are being honest with themselves. They are avowedly non-political. As persons admit their hurts, they heal. As they heal, they become stronger. As they become stronger, they self-sacrifice to the benefit of others. In addition, as they give away, they get back what they have let go. Recovery groups facilitate freedom and the gifting of self to others in the sharing of life's experience.

Life is too short and precious to be carrying so much baggage that crimps or prevents enjoyment of the journey with other healthy, brave adventurers like you.

CHAPTER ONE

INDIVIDUATION ACROSS THE LIFESPAN

"There is an appointed time for everything, and a time for every affair under the heavens. A time to be born, and a time to die; a time to plant, and a time to uproot the plant" (Ecclesiastes 3: 1-2).

Individuation is the self-realization of each person brought about through a continuing, rigorous examination, exploration, and integration of unconscious material into conscious awareness and into one's lived experience. This invitation to greater wholeness, often experienced as a "life-crisis," is most acutely experienced in mid-life. This process by which a person becomes a psychological "individual"— that is, a separate, indivisible unity or whole—is often the result of a painful "re-birth." Living a life that is the expression of one's own uniqueness is the mark of the individuated person.

Individuation, sometimes called "self-actualization," refers to that process of becoming one's very best self. This is the goal of human living. At birth, one leaves the womb to become a distinct person in the world. During the first few years of life, infants and toddlers take the first steps towards "individuation" by establishing a boundary between

1

their own selves and their parents. As individuation progresses, one gains a greater sense of who one is and what's needed and wanted.

The more one becomes individuated, the more one connects with others and the natural world. As an individuating person, one increasingly takes responsibility for the personal construction of meaning. I recall having a conversation with an adult friend about the "Holy Trinity." My friend was an ordained priest. I was a teenager at the time. I could neither understand the concept nor accept the definition of this mystery as he explained it to me. My friend insisted that I accept the doctrine if I were interested in referring to myself as a believer in good standing. I felt uneasy with this quick ticket to good standing within the orthodox faith community. As the car rolled towards the traffic light, I decided to jump out and find my way to my destination by my own means. As a teenager, it seemed that there was more involved in faith than accepting traditional doctrine without truly understanding it or finding it meaningful.

Carl Jung introduced the psychological notion of individuation. He was convinced that the advancement of culture and society depended on the degree to which each person in that culture or society individuated. Jung opposed organized religion and other large-scale programs and practices aimed at shaping and reforming individuals. He observed that such efforts resulted in wars which had drained his native Europe for centuries. Jung suspected that social organizations (like organized churches or political parties) tended to promote individualism, to encourage their members to opt for roles that are socially compensated and rewarded, but at the cost of one's own self-realization. For Jung, the development of the individual personality formed the noblest human achievement. He felt that organized religion often distracted from this journey. It was as if he thought, "Leave poor Jesus alone. Through all that wandering in the desert, Jesus looked deeply into his own shadow. He recognized God in himself. He demonstrated God through action. Follow his example. Be careful of people who outline what to do to be like Jesus. In the desert of your own experience, figure it out for yourself."

While working towards individuation is achieved on the solitary road to self-discovery, the individuating person is not anti-social. By giving honest and close scrutiny to the material emerging into one's consciousness, it becomes clear that one is united with every other human being. Each is no better, no worse than the other. Such self-examination enables one to be prepared to participate in life free from fear and social anxiety. One is less vulnerable to the mongers of hate and fear that fill our airwaves and keep persons divided one from another based on ethnicity, gender, class, and religion. One begins to recognize that the individual, not society, is the primary bearer of social life. One can make a difference because one is capable of becoming an expert in one's own experience. The more individuated and self-actualized that one becomes, the healthier the circle of relationships and the society and culture will be in which we all live.

According to Jung, the age of forty corresponds to the season of a person's life wherein one is uniquely confronted with the challenge of individuation. He writes that at about the age of forty, a person "wholly unprepared takes a step into the afternoon of life." He continues: "We take this step with the false presupposition that our truths and ideals will serve us as hitherto. But we cannot live the afternoon of life according to the program of life's morning—for what was great in the morning will be little at evening, and what in the morning was true will at the evening become a lie." Jung observed that this developmental process common to adults around the age of forty can lead to individuation or despair. It is only because of such experience that one becomes most uniquely one's own person.

Individuation in the Jungian sense does not signify an American-style individualism. Individualism refers to ego-oriented, idiosyncratic ways of thinking and behaving that tend to fragment the person and human experience. "Individualism," writes Joseph Campbell, means

3

"deliberately stressing and giving prominence to some supposed peculiarity rather than to collective considerations and obligations." For Jung, individualism represented the divesting of one's unique self in favor of an external role or imagined meaning. Individuation, on the other hand, represents the acceptance and promotion of one's innermost and incomparable uniqueness. As a form of self-realization, it implies an ongoing process towards achieving selfhood. Salvation is not a noun but a verb.

Writing during the time of Hitler's consolidation of power, Jung observed that education of adult populations conducted by organized religion resulted in a kind of conformity which made "group think" inevitable. He witnessed pastors, priests, and upper clergy urging the imitation of Christ's life while at the same time failing to underscore the purpose of Christ's life as symbol. For Jung, Christ symbolized the human life fully and uniquely lived. So, too, each person is called to self-exploration toward the discovery of his or her unique way of representing the divine in the world. To become "like Christ" as others defined him was not necessarily to bring any new insight to the human experience. Every person is challenged to explore one's own relationship to evil and good and to find the Divine in one's own self.

"The psychological rule," writes Jung, "says that when an inner situation is not made conscious, it occurs outside as fate. When the individual remains undivided and does not become conscious of his or her inner opposite, the world must perforce act out the conflict and be torn into opposing halves." The "shadow" is everything within the person that is unconscious, repressed, undeveloped, and denied. The first thing one must undertake in order to see one's shadow side is take complete responsibility for one's life. The honest effort to explore the contents of one's own shadow will lead to a deeper degree of social relatedness and social participation. The individuating person is as much self-determined as other-related. The individuating person takes personal responsibility for social realities that impact upon his or her life.

Individualism, by contrast, promotes mass-mindedness and conformity. Harry Spect criticized members of his own social work profession, calling them "unfaithful angels." He condemned the promotion of individualism as a way of economically surviving in a health care environment driven by the free market. "For-profit" insurance companies and other health maintenance organizations have sometimes appeared to make mental disorders, compulsive behaviors, and other growing societal ills into private failures.

I recently counseled a family where the father recently returned from two tours of combat duty in Iraq. Following his reentry into the family home, this ex-combatant's nine year old daughter was proving to be both oppositional and withdrawn. She met the DSM VI criteria for "oppositional defiant disorder." The father had no insurance and was unable to pay for services for his own therapy. However, he did have private insurance for his children. In calling the insurance company for an authorization to treat the child, I learned that the company drew a distinction between "serious" and "non-serious" mental illness. If the child were diagnosed with depression, this mental illness is considered a "serious" mental health condition and services would be authorized and compensated at one rate. If the same child were diagnosed with oppositional-defiant disorder, then it would be considered a "non-serious" mental health condition. Depending upon the particulars of the insurance policy, treatment for depression may be authorized, but treatment for anxiety may not be covered. The child's parents expressed their concern that if their child was diagnosed with a serious mental illness, future access to health insurance might be jeopardized or priced in such a way that it was not affordable. The real issue not being addressed was the father's unhealed experience of trauma and his daughter's brave opposition to his unwitting recreation of trauma in their family circle. The child's symptoms reflected a healthy resistance to a vicarious experience of post-traumatic stress resulting from her father's wartime service.

Social variables connected to an individual's inability to function are often ignored in health care. Depression, compulsions, and various forms of unhealthy behavior and feeling states may be ameliorated by psychotropic medications, but such treatments may only mask or obscure the true nature of these symptoms as invitations to individuation. Individuation means becoming an "in-dividual" and, as such, analogously reflects a kind of birthing process, an experience both painful and frightening.

"Anxiety," notes Rollo May, "is freedom knocking." While the age of forty is a critical time in the individuation process, other philosophers and social scientists point out that individuation is a life-long task that takes different shapes at different moments. No life structure is permanent. Periodic change is given within the nature of human existence. In the words of Cardinal John Henry Newman, "To be human, here below, is to change, and to be perfect is to change often."

CHAPTER 2

JOURNAL WRITING

"People are only as sick as the secrets they keep" is a phrase that most people in recovery have heard. Life-threatening events often come wrapped in shame and guilt. There is little desire, willingness, or knowledge as to how to process unpleasant, hurtful, life-threatening experiences. But what happens if one does not process his or her life experiences? The subconscious mind will provide a meaning to such experiences that may be the ingredients that underlie addictive and other compulsive behaviors.

The human psyche is made up of layers. The *ego* is the term Freud gave to the conscious mind. The ego represents conscious perceptions, thoughts, memories, and feelings. Mental content that threatens the ego falls into the personal unconscious. Trauma in the form of repressed, suppressed, or forgotten material is stored in the personal unconscious. Like Freud, Jung believed the human psyche was made up of both the conscious and unconscious mind. Jung went further than Freud by suggesting a further division of the unconscious mind into a personal and collective unconscious. While everyone has a personal unconscious, the collective unconscious predates the personal unconscious. The *shadow* refers to material that is repressed and isolated from consciousness. Everyone has a shadow side. The less it is incorporated into the individual's conscious life, the more likely this dark material may burst forth suddenly in a moment of unawareness. Knowing the content of one's shadow is a painstaking affair. Jung believed that in each person "there is another whom we do not know." He saw dreams as the "royal road to the unconscious." Dreams formed the bridge to both the personal and collective unconscious. Dream work is central to the process of individuation.

Recall the biblical story of Adam and Eve. They were in the Garden of Eden in the Book of Genesis, surrounded by animals that had no names. God tells them: "Name them and have dominion over them." In the scriptures, to name something is to have power and dominion over that thing. So, too, with one's experiences: "Name them, and have dominion over them." If one does not name one's trauma, those experiences and relationships that are less than nurturing have the capacity to have one cornered.

Many forms of journal writing exist. Journal writing is one of the most effective, safest ways of naming one's experiences. It is more than keeping a diary, when one records daily events and happenings from a detached point of view. Journal writing is the act of writing down thoughts and feelings in order to sort through problems and come to a deeper understanding of oneself and the issues in one's life. Journaling takes one to the core of one's deepest self. As pen meets paper or fingers touch the keyboard, each person can connect with one's own deeper self and with his or her recollections and experiences at a deep level. Journal writing is not a place for expounding upon ideas or theories. Rather, the journal is a place where one can spend time with his or her own self. Writing forms an occasion to visit an inner world where one's feelings, visions, dreams, and needs lie. The journal is the place where one can take off one's mask and put aside one's "persona." Journaling is a sacred event where each can own his or her humanness, brokenness, and trauma.

Thomas Merton once commented that he could identify a saint just by the way the person picked up a piece of paper. Throughout each day, all kinds of things happen. Most times, one is unaware of the meaning ascribed to these events. As people move through each day, reacting to people, places, and things, there may be little intentionality and attention paid in regard to people's day-to-day interactions.

Journal writing is the simple process of staying with an event. With pen in hand, or while sitting at the computer, you are able to dwell with situations and feelings. You permit yourself to be present to your experience. In a spontaneous stream of consciousness, what one feels and thinks becomes clear, real, and present. People stay with what they are describing for as long as needed, until the well runs dry, until the cup is emptied. Journal writing does not need to bring closure or ultimate resolution to whatever one is exploring. What matters is that what is inside one finds expression.

An example: I recently went to El Salvador to celebrate the *quincieñera* of my daughter. We took a taxi in downtown San Salvador to buy souvenirs. The central market for crafts is housed in an old army barracks, divided into small shops where dozens of stalls display their wares. As my family walked through the store, I listened as sellers wrangled over prices with tourists. I felt myself overwhelmed by so much activity: the crush of people walking in the streets selling produce and other goods; the ceaseless stream of buses; the loud music advertising the sale of CDs; young women carrying bags of charcoal atop their heads; young men pushing wheelbarrows piled high with trash through the clogged streets. That evening, I shared with my wife Ana that I needed to go off alone somewhere in order to process what I had seen, thought, and felt. I sensed that I needed to write with very little clarity about what I needed to write. The next day, I hopped Bus #2 and went downtown to the Cathedral of Our Savior. I sat in the cavernous church and let myself settle in and connect with what was going on inside me. Years ago, I sat in this same church near the buried remains of Archbishop Romero, the assassinated archbishop of San Salvador. I gradually took up my journal and began imagining a conversation with Monseñor Romero. I shared with him what this return trip to El Salvador meant to me. From that beginning place, I moved with whatever came to me. I wrote for an hour, simply moving with what was stirring inside me. At the end of my dialogue with Oscar Romero, I felt "emptied out."

I share this example to illustrate the importance of becoming aware of one's inner stirrings. In our hyperactive culture, we tend to ignore such stirrings, or to dismiss them as unimportant, or at least as less important than what we are occupied with at the moment. Had I moved from buying souvenirs to watching life lived out on the streets of San Salvador to celebrating the *Quinciañera,* or "sweet sixteen," of my daughter, I would eventually have reached a point of feeling inwardly cluttered and even numb. My own creativity and resiliency would have been blocked. I chose to move with what was stirring inside of me, with what was grabbing and capturing my attention. In so doing, I could be alive and present to my wife Ana and her family; to our children and to my "eschatological family" in Zacamíl, those to whom I am not related by blood, but by affection and affiliation.

Writing also enabled me to let go of some harsh memories. Often, feelings with regards to diverse situations, past and present, swirl within us constantly. One may wonder if the feelings associated with some painful experiences will ever go away. One may not be able to find a way to let go of a specific situation that stirs deep feelings. Writing in one's journal is a concrete means of helping to process what one is experiencing and, eventually, to let go of the situation, the event, the person. The letting-go process does not happen overnight. One may have to write over and over until he or she may come to an inner sense of "having gotten it all out."

"From this perspective," writes Dr. Vincent Bilotta, "journal writing is a discipline." This is especially true when you are in pain. Staying with painful inner stirrings, difficult situations, or hurtful memories is not easy. Most often, you want to put the pain aside and "get on with life." However, walking through the pain in one's journal can eventually be a source of healing, of inner resolution and growth towards individuation. Trust the journaling process. One begins by quietly knowing that as one lets down and gives oneself over to the process, his or her pain will ease and he or she will move beyond it to some new place of insight, freedom, and joy.

Finally, the journal is a place to explore, to wrestle with, and to work through insights and awareness that come to one. As one writes, he or she gains new insight and awareness. The journal is a place to describe one's sexual fantasies, where one can describe and be with one's dreams. If one feels betrayed by his or her father or feels rage with his or her mother, it may be unwise and unhelpful to express these feelings directly to one's parents! (Even in old age, one may still have parents and still might feel such things towards them). The journal provides each with the time and space to express what one is feeling as if one were talking to that person. Such expression often brings relief, as the images are no longer swirling around inside. Through writing, each has the capacity to take himself outside of himself or herself. While this is sacred material, it is not intended for the eyes of others. Confidentiality and privacy must be preserved and protected.

Part of the formative experience of our American culture, and of certain Christian preachers, had been to categorize feelings and experiences into right and wrong, good or bad, acceptable or not acceptable. This dualistic, judgmental approach to human feelings and experience, deeply ingrained in most of us, can be an obstacle to journal writing. Gradually letting go of one's judgmental approach to one's experience and feelings forms part of the discipline of journal writing. First, one should gradually try to become aware of the feelings and experiences that one tends to judge negatively. Each ought to try to set out to articulate and concretize such judgments in his or her journal.

Like all forms of discipline, journal writing requires perseverance. One's journal writing will lead one within, into one's world of feelings, memories, needs, and unresolved issues. Such a process can be threatening. In our fast-paced, consumer-oriented society; we are bombarded with one image after another. Neither discipline nor the journey within is greatly valued. Many resist the challenges and opportunities of journal writing and need to address this dynamic in their journals. By listening to and journaling about the dynamic of resistance, one can become clearer about it. Owning that resistance and befriending it will enable one to move beyond it. It may move each person to be more healthy and productive and to a more healing place.

CHAPTER 3

AUTOBIOGRAPHY: SACRED HISTORY

As part of the individuation process, consider now the unique journey through which each person has been formed. The writing of one's personal story is an integrative process of reflecting upon his or her personal history and tracing the various threads that form the woven tapestry that is called one's story.

Begin to listen with the inner ear to the people, events, and things that have contributed to one's formative story.... Take up the remembering process in a spirit of openness and receptivity to the significant people, events, and things that have become an integral part of the mystery of what one is.

Sit down. Slow down. Set aside time for reverence, respect, gentleness, compassion, and humility. This exercise is not an analytical introspection, but rather, a process of gradually appreciating the uniqueness of one's sacred personal story in light of the ongoing unfolding of the creation story in which we are all involved.

The autobiography you are invited to write may be structured into the following chapters:

1. Paternal grandparents

2. Maternal grandparents

3. Parents

4. One's parents' relationship

5. One's relationship with his or her mother

6. One's relationship to his or her father

7. One's relationship to his or her brothers and sisters

8. Family patterns

9. Educational periods

10. Relationship to oneself

11. Relationship to others

12. Relationship to God

13. Sexuality

14. Reflective integration

Treat each section as a separate chapter in one's life story. Be as specific and concrete as possible in descriptions. Use as many adjectives as possible, but don't worry about the exactness of grammar, writing style, sentence structure, vocabulary, etc. Through this autobiography, one will paint a picture of who one has been, who one is now, and where one is going.

As one begins one's autobiography, he or she can try to describe how one feels as each specific chapter begins. What did one feel as he or she read the chapter title? How did he or she feel while completing each chapter? Note, too, any moments of frustration, resistance, sadness, joy, gratitude, negativity, tiredness, confusion, and so on.

An autobiography is, in fact, sacred history. It is the "stuff" that makes one who he or she is. Reflecting on one's story and writing it down, each can become better grounded in who one is, and to befriend the unique mystery of whom one is and how one is moving towards individuation.

I.   Paternal Grandparents

Please describe a portrait of your paternal grandparents. This should be presented not from your perspective but from your father's perspective. If available, include the following information:

A. Ages, dates of birth and death, ethnicity, place born, places reared, occupations, educational levels, medical problems, emotional and mental health, personality traits, description of marriage relationship over the years.

B. Describe the story of the rearing of their children: List the names, sexes, and ages of their children in chronological order, places born, years of births and deaths, marriages, divorces, places reared, occupations, educational levels, medical problems over the years, and emotional and mental health over the years, personality traits, and your father's relationship to each of his siblings over the years.

C. Describe any themes, myths, values, rules, misfortunes, tragedies, transitions, and accomplishments of this generation of extended family characters and events.

D. Describe your relationship with your paternal grandparents. What memories exist about them? What feelings are recalled from being around them? How did they relate to the journal writer? Are they currently living or deceased? What is the current relationship to them? If deceased, what was the experience of their death like for the journal keeper and for his or her family?

E. E. Were any paternal extended family members significant during your formative years (aunts, uncles, cousins, grandparents)? Portray in what way they were significant in your life. What is your current relationship with this (these) person(s)?

II. Maternal Grandparents

Please provide a portrait of your maternal grandparents. This picture should be presented not from your perspective, but from your mother's perspective. If available, include the following information:

A. Ages, dates of births and deaths, ethnicity, places born, places reared, occupations, educational levels, medical problems, emotional health, personality traits, description of marriage relationship.

B. Describe the story of the rearing of their children: List the names, sexes, and ages of their children in chronological order, years of births and deaths, marriages, divorces, places reared, occupation, educational levels, medical problems over the years, and emotional health over the years, personality traits, and the mother's relationship to each of her siblings.

C. Describe any themes, myths, values, rules, misfortunes, tragedies, transitions, and accomplishments of this generation of extended family characters and events.

D. Describe your relationship with the maternal grandparents. What memories do you have about them? How did you feel around them? How did they relate to the journal keeper? Are they currently living or deceased? What is your current relationship with them? If deceased, what was the experience of their death like for yourself and your family?

E. Were any maternal extended family members significant during your growing up years (aunts, uncles, cousins, grandparents)? Describe in what way they were significant in your formative years. What is your current relationship with this (these) person(s)?

III. Parents

Let's now move on and focus on your nuclear family.

A. Describe, as concretely as possible, your father's story from his birth to the time he began to court the journal keeper's mother. In particular, please describe how your father was shaped, formed, influenced by his father, mother, siblings, birth order in the family, the school system, his religion, and so forth.

B. Describe, as concretely as possible, your mother's story from her birth to the time she began to be courted by your father. In particular, please describe how the journal keeper's mother was shaped, formed, influenced by her father, mother, siblings, birth order in the family, the school system, religion, and so forth.

IV. Parents' Relationship

A. At some point in time, the journal keeper's parents became engaged and married. Please describe the situation and events of their marriage relationship. In what year did they start their courtship? When and where did they marry? In what years were their children born? Supply years of miscarriages, deaths of any of the children, years of any serious illnesses or hospitalizations, years of any job losses, moves, and major dislocations or transitions within the family.

B. Describe how the parents related to each other over the years. Characterize their relationship over time. What kind of marriage did they have? How did they deal with the following as a couple: household chores, feelings of anger towards each other, decision-making, conflicts, finances, control, affection, rest and relaxation, stress, holidays, vacations, limit-setting with their children, family crisis, their parents' deaths, and dialogue with each other? What were the values and rules that they lived as a couple while their children were growing up?

V. One's Relationship to One's Mother

A. Describe the mother physically. What was the quality of her energy over the years (high, low, vibrant, depressed, endurance, enthusiasm)?

B. Describe the relationship with your mother over the years (include special moments, issues of trust, support, affirmation, respect, playing, leisure time, responsibility, traditions, rituals, values that one shared or was in conflict about).

C. What did you enjoy doing with your mother? What did she enjoy doing with each child? What were you in conflict about over the years with your mother?

D. Was there anything about the mother that you feared? How did this fear affect each child and you, and how did you deal with it?

E. How did the mother deal with her anger towards the journal keeper?

F. How did the journal keeper deal with his or her anger towards his or her mother?

G. How did the mother disappoint the journal keeper?

H. How did the journal keeper disappoint his or her mother?

I. In what ways did the mother and journal keeper hurt each other over the years, and how have those hurts been dealt with, resolved, or healed over the years?

J. How did the mother handle issues of authority, control, and independence in the family?

VI. One's Relationship to One's Father

A. Describe the journal keeper's father physically. What was the quality of his energy over the years (high, low, vibrant, depressed, endurance, enthusiasm)?

B. Describe the relationship with your father over the years (include special moments, issues of trust, support, affirmation, respect, playing, leisure time, responsibility, traditions, rituals, values that one shared or were in conflict).

C. What did the journal keeper enjoy doing with his or her father? What did he enjoy doing with the journal keeper? What were the conflicts experienced with the father over the years?

D. Was there anything about the journal keeper's father that he or she feared? How did this fear affect the family members, and how did each one deal with it?

E. How did the father deal with his anger towards the journal keeper?

F. How did the journal keeper deal with his or her anger towards his or her father?

G. How did the father disappoint the journal keeper?

H. How did the journal keeper disappoint his or her father?

I. In what ways did each hurt the other over the years, and how have those hurts been dealt with over the years?

J. How did the father handle issues of authority, control, and independence in the family?

VII. Brothers and Sisters

A. Describe the relationship to each brother and sister over the years.

B. Describe your birth order in the family and in what way this birth order influenced the development of aspects of your personality.

C. Who was the hero in the family? Why?

D. Who was the scapegoat in the family? Why?

E. Who was the lost child in the family? Why?

F. Who was the rebel in the family? Why?

G. Who was the mascot in the family? Why?

H. Most siblings develop some rivalry with each other. Please describe the experience of rivalry among any of the brothers and sisters.

I. For whom is the journal keeper named? Why? What is known about that person's story?

VIII. Family Patterns

A. Please describe how discipline was carried out in the journal keeper's family. Was it the same for each sibling? If not, how did it differ? Did one or both parents get involved in the discipline?

B. Please read this statement: "I recall a time when I really upset Mom." Describe the situation. What did she say? What did she do? What did the journal keeper do in response? Now, close your eyes and recall the situation as vividly as possible, then write a description of it, including factual recollections and those on a feeling basis.

C. Please read this statement: "I recall a time when I really upset Dad." Describe the situation. What did he say? What did he do? What did the journal writer do in response? Now, close your eyes and recall the situation as vividly as possible, then write a description.

D. Did the mother have a pet saying? If so, what was it?

E. Did the father have a pet saying? If so, what was it?

F. Please describe from one's observations and experience the family patterns of celebration, ritual, values, conflicts, and experiences that unfolded as part of the family's story at Christmas, Thanksgiving, Easter, birthdays and other significant holidays; Sundays and weekends.

G. Imagine the layout of the apartment or house in which the family lived.

H. Describe the important places in these family spaces. In what room did the family spend most of its time?

I. Describe the patterns of the following everyday events in the family that occurred over the years.

   1. What was waking up in the morning like for the family members?

   2. What was lunch like for the family?

   3. What was after school like for the family?

   4. What was supper like for the family?

   5. What was bedtime like for the family?

   6. What were Sundays like for the family?

   7. What were vacations like for the family?

J. Did the journal keeper live in more than one place during his or her formative years? If so, describe each move; the reasons for the move(s); your age and grade level at the time of each move; and the impact of each move upon you and your family. How did the journal keeper and family adjust to each move, to a change of community, of school, of neighborhood?

IX. Educational Periods

A. Describe the primary school story. Please address remembrances of the first day of school, your relationship with your teachers, relationships with the boys, relationships with the girls, recess periods, significant successes and failures, interests, and involvements in grammar school. Write about experiences with sports.

B. Describe high school story memories. Please address this in relationship to your teachers, peers (male and female), interests, and involvements in high school. How was time spent during the summers in high school?

C. Describe your undergraduate college experience.

X. Relationship to Oneself

A. What is the general state of the journal keeper's health? Were there any health problems over the years? If so, describe them. How have these problems been handled? How are they currently being treated?

B. Have you had any previous experiences of counseling or therapy? What precipitated these experiences? For what period of time did the journal keeper remain in therapy? What insights and awareness were gained from this experience?

C. Given all that you have written thus far in your autobiography, please describe who you see yourself to be as a human being. (Include your strengths and weakness, what you need to change about yourself, how you deal with your feelings of anger and hurt, your hobbies and interests, your successes and failures, how you deal with stress, conflicts, making decisions, relaxation, free time, work, and ways of helping yourself to develop and grow as a human being).

XI. Relationship to Others

A. Describe your relationships to men, women, and persons in authority

B. Describe your style of helping others.

C. Describe your history of working on and with a team.

D. Describe your experience of working with and/or being with difficult people.

E. Describe your relationship with one of your friends.

F. Describe particular areas of conflicts that stylistically develop with other people.

XII. Relationship to God

A. Describe your story of your relationship to you Higher Power, however you imagine it.

B. In what ways, if any, do you image God?

C. Where do you experience silence and solitude in everyday life?

D. Describe the personal style of prayer or meditation, if any.

E. In what way do you take up sacred scripture or another source of inspiration in daily life?

F. What are your experiences of involvement in activities that serve the needs of others?

G. Describe key moments in life that have given shape and direction to your faith development.

H. How do you handle anger with God?

I. Describe key persons that have given shape and direction to your faith development. Describe in what way they were significant in this regard.

J. Describe what hopes, values, and dreams are directing your life at this time.

XIII. Sexuality

A. Describe your sexual orientation, attractions, and history.

XIV. Reflective Integration

A. In this chapter, please go back and reread all previous thirteen chapters and your journal entries in regard to the process of writing this autobiography. After getting a feel for the flow of your life over the years, please write a brief reflection about who you are in the present and who you hope to become in the future. Also, describe the areas of gratitude and appreciation in your life and the residual, negative, unresolved conflicts that you need to work on in the months to come.

CHAPTER 4

TRAUMA AND STORYTELLING

You have written your autobiography. You can plainly see that your life, like every life, contains some mixture of order and disorder, unity and diversity, integration and fragmentation. Life is always flawed in some respects. In these flaws lie your treasure.

Trauma is any experience that is non-nurturing. In this context, trauma is synonymous with abuse. It does not matter whether a particular experience was intentional or not. It is only important to name one's experience. As you read over your personal story, consider the following definitions:

Webster's dictionary defines *abandonment* as "to withdraw protection, support, or help." Is abandonment a part of your experience? Were your parents or major care givers absent from your life, either physically or emotionally? Did your parents fail to intervene or protect you from abuse? Were your parents absent because of workaholism? Did it seem that you spent many hours in daycare? Did illness or injury limit the time your mother or father could spend with the family when you were growing up? Was the communication between the parents and the journal keeper poor? In an effort to get their needs met, did the parents enmesh with one another? Was it necessary for the journal keeper to put aside his or her true self, his or her inner child, to play a part that the family system needed in order to survive? Did the journal keeper experience apathy or outright rejection as a child? Was he or she ever forgotten about and left in a car seat, a crib, or a swing? These are all forms of abandonment. Remember, if one can get in touch with such experiences and tell stories about them, one can experience healing.

Neglect is defined as the failure to provide for a child's physical survival needs to the extent that there is harm or risk of harm to the child's health or safety. This may include, but is not limited to, lack of supervision; lack of adequate nutrition that places the child below the normal growth curve; lack of shelter; or lack of medical or dental care that results in health-threatening conditions. The dictionary defines *neglect* as giving "little attention or respect." As a child, did you experience neglect? Did the journal keeper eat good-quality food? Did he or she get enough to eat? Did he or she receive quality medical and dental care? Was he or she taught how to care properly for his or her body? Did he or she get enough sleep? Did the parents or guardians show appropriate affection? Was the journal keeper hugged, held, rocked? Did those around play with the journal keeper? Did he or she get a sense that the parents or guardians enjoyed being around the journal keeper? Did he or she ever receive the message, "I do not want anyone to touch me"?

Abuse can be defined as an improper or excessive intervention. Physical abuse may be defined as any act which, regardless of intent, results in a non-accidental physical injury. Inflicted physical injury most often represents unreasonably severe corporal punishment. This usually happens when the parent is frustrated or angry and strikes, shakes, or throws the child.

Sexual abuse is defined as acts of sexual assault and sexual exploitation of minors. Sexual abuse encompasses a broad range of behavior and may consist of many acts over a long period of time or a single incident.

The nature of sexual abuse, the shame of the child victim, and the possible involvement of trusted parents, stepparents, or other persons in a caretaker role make it extremely difficult for children to come forward to report sexual abuse.

Emotional abuse includes verbal assaults, ignoring, and indifference or constant family conflict. If a child is degraded enough, the child will begin to live up to the image communicated by the abusing parent or caretaker.

Child abuse can happen anywhere: in poor, middle-class, or well-to-do homes, in rural or urban areas. The present reflection is not intended as a debate about "effectiveness" of physical punishment. As one reads through the following list, only consider if these things actually occurred. As the journal keeper acknowledges the experience, he or she ought to be attentive to his or her personal feelings:

Was the journal keeper hit or punched as a child? Was he or she slapped in the face, kicked, choked, or shaken? Was he or she pulled by the arm, shoved into a wall, or held down against his or her will? With what objects were you hit, if any: a fly swatter, wire hanger, hairbrush, shoe, belt, leash, electrical cord, wooden spoon, ping-pong paddle, etc.?

Was the journal keeper told: "Go to your room—I cannot stand to look at you now," or "Just wait until your father comes home"? Was the journal keeper made to eat soap, Tabasco sauce, hot peppers? Was he or she forced to smoke or forced to drink to teach him or her a lesson? Was he or she given an enema often for unexplained reasons?

When parents are overly critical or needy, boundaries blur and emotional abuse often results. Consider the following: has the journal keeper witnessed the abuse of siblings? Has the journal keeper been punished or shamed for expressing his or her feelings as a child? Was he or she taught not to express his or her emotions appropriately? Was one taught moderation and containment? Was one forced to act like an adult before becoming one? Was the journal keeper belittled or demeaned? Was he or she given the silent treatment? Was he or she compared unfavorably to his or her siblings, classmates, and friends? Did the one parent and the other compete between themselves for the attention of the journal writer? Was the journal writer burdened with the requirement to carry many family secrets? Did the parents make such comments as, "We are only staying together because of you"? Was the journal keeper ever threatened with suicide or homicide?

Intellectual abuse occurs when a child's thinking and reality are attacked. Did the journal keeper's parents demand perfection? Did they expect an all-out effort to be put forth all of the time? Conversely, did one's major care givers never expect excellence? Did the journal keeper move habitually from school to school? Was he or she set up to fail by being required to attend a specific school? Was he or she taught problem solving? Did he or she have a learning disability? Was he or she teased in school? Was he or she diagnosed with Attention Deficit Disorder or with any other behavioral or mental health labels? Did the parents or major care givers read to the journal keeper or help with the homework? Were the journal keeper's ideas sought and respected? Was he or she ever segregated by teachers, coaches, or administrators?

One's sexuality is one of the most sacred aspects of who he or she is. Sexual abuse can be overt or covert. Examples of covert or hidden sexual abuse are rampant in our society. Every time a girl or boy is objectified to sell clothes, food, or a television program, sexual abuse occurs. When children reach the age of puberty wholly unaware of what changes are occurring with their maturing bodies, this can be experienced as abuse. Did one of the journal keeper's major care givers attempt to explain to him or her about the wonders of his or her sexual self? Was he or she prepared for the changes that adolescence brought? Was sexual education information provided to the journal keeper in a developmentally appropriate way? Was the information accurate? (Overt sexual abuse refers to any sexual contact between an adult and a child. This is always the responsibility of the adult).

Since all abuse is not about truth and love, all abuse has spiritual effects. It affects the way one perceives oneself, others, and the divine. Did one's parents or primary caregivers make themselves one's Higher Power? Did the journal keeper experience the demeaning of other faiths and beliefs? Were religious beliefs forced upon him or her? Did the journal keeper ever experience abuse at the hands of a religious figure? Were God or religion ever used to threaten or manipulate him or her? Did the journal keeper experience messages that women are to be viewed as somehow less than men? Was he or she given the message that he or she was a grave sinner or that he or she would burn in hell? Has he or she ever been involved with witchcraft, exorcisms, or other occult practices? Was he or she provided with no spiritual framework at all? Did the journal keeper experience rejection for his or her spiritual beliefs? Was he or she persecuted or judged on account of race, gender or sexual orientation?

The goal here is to acknowledge these experiences if they happened. These experiences can make one healthy, wealthy, and wise ... or they can be submerged into one's shadow side to be quietly forgotten, but perversely played out in relationships marked by turmoil and inadequate boundaries.

CHAPTER FIVE

THE MENTORING RELATIONSHIP

Telling one's story is a concrete way of connecting with one's roots. One can begin to discover who he or she is as member of one's specific family, religious community, and culture. Telling one's story sounds simple. After all, the journal keeper is an expert in his or her own experience, as one has been living one's story for one's whole life! But sometimes, it is difficult to begin to tell one's own story. Who wants to listen? It's easy to dismiss the idea. "That's the way it was," one may have said. "It's no big deal." Or, "So what? There's nothing special about my story." "What difference will it make, anyway?" And, after all, "Who cares, anyway?" Let me preface this by acknowledging the human tendency to rationalize, to make errors, and to fool ourselves. So rather than paint this exercise as replete with reliability and validity, let me say instead that this part of the "coming home" exercise is meant to be both interesting and fun.

It starts with the belief that one's story is sacred history. The struggles, pains, and suffering that one has acknowledged form the stuff of wisdom. One's experiences and the meaning to be discovered in them are the marks of raised consciousness and new awareness. One's experiences are unique and supply the keys to one's individuation process. Just as the Hebrew prophets emerged from the desert to speak new truth to the world, to witness to the divine in some new way, so, too, one's personal experiences remain to teach and guide self … and others. (Recall that in their lifetimes, the prophets and their messages were not exactly well received … for the most part). So, before finding a counselor to help one frame one's story, think of a mentor: someone with whom one's story can be shared.

When I was young, I would sit with my journal and dialogue, in my imagination, with the person of Jesus. For me, Jesus was a fine mentor. With humility, I felt Jesus invited me to explore all dimensions of my life and experience. He seemed interested in how I made sense of things. Jesus seemed to be a person whose knowledge of the spiritual life came from his own hunger, trials, struggles, loneliness, and desire to make the world a better, more just place. From what I knew about Jesus, he showed concern for others. Just maybe, I figured, he might have been concerned for me as a fellow pilgrim. Jesus was a person who showed respect for all people without distinction. He was honest in challenging the wise as well as the ignorant; the poor as well as the wealthy; the healthy as well as the sick.

Jesus is not the only wise person, however. Consider the following quotes from wisdom figures that have gone before us:

Dr. Martin Luther King
(1929-1968)

All progress is precarious. We may have all come on different ships, but we're in the same boat now.

The solution of one problem brings us face to face with another problem.

An individual who breaks a law that conscience tells him is unjust, and who willingly accepts the penalty of imprisonment in order to arouse the conscience of the community over its injustice, is in reality expressing the highest respect for the law.

Change does not roll in on the wheels of inevitability, but comes through continuous struggle. And so we must straighten our backs and work for our freedom. A man can't ride you unless your back is bent.

Darkness cannot drive out darkness; only light can do that. Hate cannot drive out hate; only love can do that.

Every man must decide whether he will walk in the light of creative altruism or in the darkness of destructive selfishness.

Everything that we see is a shadow cast by that which we do not see.

Faith is taking the first step even when you don't see the whole staircase.

Freedom is never voluntarily given by the oppressor; it must be demanded by the oppressed.

A genuine leader is not a searcher for consensus but a molder of consensus.

A nation that continues year after year to spend more money on military defense than on programs of social uplift is approaching spiritual doom.

A right delayed is a right denied.

A riot is at bottom the language of the unheard.

Almost always, the creative, dedicated minority has made the world better.

An individual has not started living until he can rise above the narrow confines of his individualistic concerns to the broader concerns of all humanity.

At the center of non-violence stands the principle of love

Discrimination is a hellhound that gnaws at Negroes in every waking moment of their lives to remind them that the lie of their inferiority is accepted as truth in the society dominating them

Have we not come to such an impasse in the modern world that we must love our enemies—or else? The chain reaction of evil—hate begetting hate, wars producing more wars—must be broken, or else we shall be plunged into the dark abyss of annihilation

He who passively accepts evil is as much involved in it as he who helps to perpetrate it. He who accepts evil without protesting against it is really cooperating with it

History will have to record that the greatest tragedy of this period of social transition was not the strident clamor of the bad people, but the appalling silence of the good people

Human progress is neither automatic nor inevitable... Every step toward the goal of justice requires sacrifice, suffering, and struggle; the tireless exertions and passionate concern of dedicated individuals.

I believe that unarmed truth and unconditional love will have the final word in reality. This is why right, temporarily defeated, is stronger than evil triumphant.

I have decided to stick with love. Hate is too great a burden to bear.

Mother Teresa
(1910-1997)

Be faithful in small things because it is in them that your strength lies

Being unwanted, unloved, uncared for, forgotten by everybody, I think that is a much greater hunger, a much greater poverty than the person who has nothing to eat

Do not think that love, in order to be genuine, has to be extraordinary. What we need is to love without getting tired

Do not wait for leaders; do it alone, person to person

Good works are links that form a chain of love

I am a little pencil in the hand of a writing God who is sending a love letter to the world

I have found the paradox, that if you love until it hurts, there can be no more hurt, only more love.

I want you to be concerned about your next door neighbor. Do you know your next door neighbor?

If we have no peace, it is because we have forgotten that we belong to each other.

If you can't feed a hundred people, then feed just one.

If you judge people, you have no time to love them.

In this life, we cannot do great things. We can only do small things with great love.

Intense love does not measure; it just gives.

It is a kingly act to assist the fallen.

It is impossible to walk rapidly and be unhappy.

Jesus said, "Love one another." He didn't say "Love the whole world."

Loneliness, and the feeling of being unwanted, is the most terrible poverty.

Love is a fruit in season at all times, and within reach of every hand.

One of the greatest diseases is to be nobody to anybody.

The success of love is in the loving—it is not in the result of loving. Of course, it is natural in love to want the best for the other person, but whether it turns out that way or not does not determine the value of what we have done.

We need to find God, and he cannot be found in noise and restlessness. God is the friend of silence. See how nature—trees, flowers, grass—grows in silence; see the stars, the moon and the sun, how they move in silence…. We need silence to be able to touch souls.

Mahatma Gandhi
(1869-1947)

As long as you derive inner help and comfort from anything, keep it.

You must not lose faith in humanity. Humanity is an ocean; if a few drops of the ocean are dirty, the ocean does not become dirty.

What difference does it make to the dead, the orphans, and the homeless, whether the mad destruction is wrought under the name of totalitarianism or the holy name of liberty or democracy?

A coward is incapable of exhibiting love; it is the prerogative of the brave.

A man is but the product of his thoughts; what he thinks, he becomes.

A religion that takes no account of practical affairs and does not help to solve them is no religion.

A small body of determined spirits fired by an unquenchable faith in their mission can alter the course of history.

A vow is a purely religious act which cannot be taken in a fit of passion. It can be taken only with a mind purified and composed and with God as witness.

Action expresses priorities.

All the religions of the world, while they may differ in other respects, unitedly proclaim that nothing lives in this world but Truth.

Always aim at complete harmony of thought and word and deed. Always aim at purifying your thoughts and everything will be well.

An eye for eye only ends up making the whole world blind.

An ounce of practice is worth more than tons of preaching.

As human beings, our greatness lies not so much in being able to remake the world—that is the myth of the atomic age—as in being able to remake ourselves.

Be the change that you want to see in the world.

Before the throne of the Almighty, man will be judged not by his acts, but by his intentions. For God alone reads our hearts.

Confession of errors is like a broom which sweeps away the dirt and leaves the surface brighter and clearer. I feel stronger for confession.

Each one has to find his peace from within. And peace, to be real, must be unaffected by outside circumstances.

Each one prays to God according to his own light. *yes*

Even if you are a minority of one, the truth is the truth.

Everyone who wills can hear the inner voice. It is within everyone.

Fear has its use, but cowardice has none.

First they ignore you; then they laugh at you; then they fight you; then you win.

Gentleness, self-sacrifice, and generosity are the exclusive possession of no one race or religion.

Oscar Romero
(1917-1980)

Those committed to the poor must share the same fate as the poor.

A church that suffers no persecution but enjoys the privileges and support of the things of the earth—beware!—is not the true church of Jesus Christ. A preaching that does not point out sin is not the preaching of the gospel. A preaching that makes sinners feel good, so that they are secured in their sinful state, betrays the gospel's call.

When the church hears the cry of the oppressed, it cannot but denounce the social structures that give rise to and perpetuate the misery from which the cry arises.

The church would betray its own love for God and its fidelity to the gospel if it stopped being ... a defender of the nights of the poor ... a humanizer of every legitimate struggle to achieve a more just society ... that prepares the way for the true reign of God in history.

I do not believe in death without resurrection. If they kill me, I will rise again in the people of El Salvador.

Aspire not to have more, but to be more.

Let us not tire of preaching love; it is the force that will overcome the world.

The poor have shown the church the true way to go. A church that does not speak out from the side of the poor is not the true church of Jesus.

The violence we preach is not the violence of the sword; … it is the violence of love.

Let my blood be a seed of freedom.

I will not tire of declaring that if we really want an effective end to violence, we must remove the violence that lies at the root of all violence: structural violence, social injustice, exclusion of citizens from the management of the country, repression. All this is what constitutes the primal cause, from which the rest flows naturally.

I'm deeply impressed by that moment when Christ stands alone before the world figured in Pilate. The truth is left alone; his own followers have been afraid. Truth is fearfully daring, and only heroes can follow the truth. So much so that Peter, who has said he will die if need be, flees like a coward and Christ stands alone.

We must not seek the child Jesus in the pretty figures of our Christmas cribs. We must seek him among the undernourished children who have gone to bed at night with nothing to eat, among the poor newsboys who will sleep covered with newspapers in doorways.

Brothers, you came from our own people. You are killing your own brothers. Any human order to kill must be subordinate to the law of God, which says, 'Thou shalt not kill.' No soldier is obliged to obey an order contrary to the law of God. No one has to obey an immoral law. It is high time you obeyed your consciences rather than sinful orders. The church cannot remain silent before such an abomination.… In the name of God, in the name of this suffering people whose cry rises to heaven more loudly each day, I implore you, I beg you, I order you: stop the repression."

And so, brothers and sisters, I repeat again what I have said here so often, addressing by radio those who perhaps have caused so many injustices and acts of violence, those who have brought tears to so many homes, those who have stained themselves with the blood of so many murders, those who have hands soiled with tortures, those who have calloused their consciences, who are unmoved to see under their boots a person abased, suffering, perhaps ready to die. To all of them I say: no matter your crimes. They are ugly and horrible, and you have abased the highest dignity of a human person, but God calls you and forgives you. And here perhaps arises the aversion of those who feel they are laborers from the first hour. How can I be in heaven with those criminals? Brothers and sisters, in heaven there are no criminals. The greatest criminal, once he has repented of his sins, is now a child of God.

Prophet Mohammed
(570-632)

Even as the fingers of the two hands are equal, so are human beings equal to one another. No one has any right, nor any preference to claim over another.

Do not consider any act of kindness insignificant, even meeting your brother with a cheerful face.

The strong man is not the good wrestler; the strong man is only the one who controls himself when he is angry

A man's true wealth hereafter is the good he does in this world to his fellow man.

The ink of the scholar is more sacred than the blood of the martyr.

Imagine some specific person whom you consider to be wise. It may be someone who is living or someone who is dead. It may be someone one known personally or someone whom one wishes to know

41

more about. It may be your father or mother. It may be a teacher from school. It may be a friend from childhood. It may be anyone who has something to teach you or with whom you might resolve some unfinished business.

Does the journal keeper have a mentor in mind? Now, add a pinch of curiosity. Since one's mentor is wise, he or she is interested in hearing the journal keeper's unique story. Begin by greeting him or her and asking this wisdom figure to accompany you and to share your story. Perhaps you will want to hear from the mentor what makes him or her tick and how he or she finds meaning in life.

In sharing one's story with one's mentor, one will become experientially aware of the shared humanity that binds both together. The journal keeper's story will move him or her from realm of his or her private world to a sense of connectedness with others. For beneath the specifics of potentially individuating circumstances, events, and life situations lies the reality of one's shared humanity. One struggles through moments of self-doubt and enjoys moments of self-confidence. One experiences success and works through failure. One struggles to make sense of his or her sexuality and integrate it into the wholeness of who he or she is. Everyone experiences the deep need to belong. Each person yearns for intimacy. He or she has attempted to hide his or her weaknesses and vulnerabilities. Everyone craves happiness. As each shares his or her story with a mentor, the awareness of his or her shared humanity may dawn, helping the seeker to become more compassionate, understanding, and gentle towards oneself and others. The journal keeper may be less frightened of the secrets that may have been controlling factors in his or her life for so long. He or she is not alone. His or her mentor has walked a similar journey, and others around the journal keeper also walk this journey, in silence, with the earnest seeker.

Life happens in a given time and place. The process of ascribing meaning always occurs in an historical context. I wish to encourage the journal keeper to dialogue with the mentor about one's own experiences against the backdrop of one's own time and place. I wish to demonstrate this by example. A therapist can only "heal" others to the extent that he or she has been healed. Carl Jung would not teach his therapeutic techniques to those unwilling or unable to move through therapy themselves. I invite the reader, then, into my world and into the experiences of living in a tiny Central American country named El Salvador.

As a Catholic missionary, I worked in Central America throughout the 1980s. The social scientist, Jesuit priest, and martyr, Martin "Nacho" Baro, wrote about the traumatization of an entire people. I learned from him and others that no one is free when others are oppressed.

Martìn Baro's life and death, along with his Jesuit colleagues and many of my Salvadoran parishioners, haunt me to this day. In an effort to gain insight and recommit myself to their healing and struggle, I employed dialogical journaling.

I offer the following example in my "conversation with the Dalai Lama."

CHAPTER SIX

CONVERSATION WITH THE DALAI LAMA

Bill: On a sultry Texas morning in 2008, Dali Lama, I just listened to an interview that you gave to the BBC. The reporter was trying to get you to say that you would be pleased if Tibet boycotted the summer 2008 Beijing Olympics. Try as he might, the reporter could not get you to admit any personal interest in leading an opposition to Red China. You described Tibet as a country of compassion. You offered the idea that if everyone were to practice compassion, in whatever the form, it would lead to worldwide changes and worldwide peace. You said, too, that the respect for human rights takes precedence over long-term economic interests.

As I sat in my car and waited for the traffic light to turn, I heard you laugh. As I listened to you, I felt something wet streak down my cheek. "Now, why am I crying?" I thought to myself. I have met people like you. Even though I do not know much about Tibetan Buddhism or about the troubles in your country following the communist takeover, I know that you are someone who can look deep within someone with eyes of love and not of judgment.

I am wondering if I can have an imaginary conversation with you. Of course, I do not really know what you would say to me as I tell you about myself and my life, but I supply you with words as I think you would answer, advise, challenge, and counsel me. Do you mind if we begin?

Dalai Lama: Bill, I would be pleased to. What would you like to discuss? Many big issues loom in the world today. You say that you have met people like me, and so I have met people like you. I know how you have come to know Dr. Martin Luther King and the way he tied militarism and the arms race to the disrespect of the individual. I know how much you honor the memory of Archbishop Oscar Romero, who was truly a brave man for his courage to change. Bill, the courage to change is the greatest courage of all. You want to speak about and reflect upon yourself and your own experiences. I do not want to do all the talking. I am capable of talking too much. If you heard me speak more, you would know this is true.

Bill: Last night, I was putting my youngest son to bed. His name, like mine, is Bill. He is six years old. Bill was having a hard time going to sleep. I pulled out my banged-up acoustical guitar. I sat at the foot of the bed and began to play a song that we sang when I was in a high school seminary: "The Lord is my shepherd." I could not see my boy in the darkened room, but I could hear his voice. "Dad," he said to me, "who is going to be my daddy when you die?"

The question caught me off guard. "Why do you ask, son?" I responded while trying to think of an age-appropriate response answer that would not traumatize him.

"You're going to die, right?" he insisted.

"Yes," I said. "This is true of all of us." I heard no sound from him, so I ventured further a bit: "Bill, we don't know when we are going to die. However, when we do, God holds us by the hand. Do not be afraid. It's certainly nothing to worry about." As I strummed the guitar, I could tell by his breathing that he had fallen asleep,

Dalai Lama: Bill, I am proud that you have chosen to share this with me.

Bill: Would you mind if I shared with you different things in my life?

Dali Lama: I am all ears, my brother.

Bill: My adventure started when I met my first mentor like yourself. His name was Fred Schafer.

Dalai Lama: A mentor is someone who teaches. Tell me: How was Fred a mentor to you?

Bill: It wasn't so much what Fred taught with words. It was his actions, his way of being in the world, that played a very important part in my life.

Dalai Lama: I'm always interested in interesting people.

Bill: Fred was the pastor at St. Brigid's in Westbury, New York. St. Brigid's is a beautiful, old stone church built by Irish immigrants. Near the church sits a railway station. Westbury is one stop removed from Hicksville, where I used to shine shoes on summer mornings when I was a boy.

Dalai Lama: Mahatma Gandhi had an awakening on a train. Were you tossed off a train for your beliefs, like he was?

Bill: It was more like being blinded by a light when I saw Fred deal with the people coming from the Long Island Railroad station.

Dalai Lama: How was that?

Bill: In the 1970s and 1980s, great unrest existed in Central America. The Catholic church had been targeted by the U.S.-backed governments as a haven for communist sympathizers. As the church proclaimed a "preferential option for the poor," Catholics were regularly targeted for persecution.

One afternoon, I sat talking with Fred when a knock came from the back door. Fred was a large man. His hands were strong, and his portly size made him loom large. *"Salud,"* I heard him say in Spanish. He opened the door.

A small Latino man with a worn suit jacket and threadbare dress pants appeared. He handed Fred a crumpled, dirty piece of paper. It had a phone number on it. He nodded his head slightly, as if in response to his own thoughts. I learned two Spanish words: *"Venga,"* he said. "Come." And then, "Come. Eat."

The man found a seat at the lengthy oak table in the rectory dining room. He excused himself and devoured a plate of spaghetti that had magically appeared. Fred waited on the man, bringing him extra bread and water. After eating, the guest spoke in hushed tones about matters which, judging from his facial expression, appeared grave. After a series of bows and several *"gracias, muchas gracias,"* the weathered man disappeared into the humid Long Island night.

Dalai Lama: Who was the man?

Bill: He was a refugee from a place called El Salvador.

Dalai Lama: And the phone number he gave?

Bill: The number was of a relative somewhere on Long Island.

Dalai Lama: So Fred was part of, how would one put it, an "underground railroad?"

Bill: Yes. On occasion, I would spend the night sleeping on a couch or in a chair or on the floor at St. Brigid's. Sometimes, one or another of the priests assigned to the parish would return home and find that Fred had given away his bed, too! There were people from El Salvador, Nicaragua, and Guatemala. Sometimes, there were people from India and Africa as well. The people who came to Westbury were refugees. All people were welcome at St. Brigid's rectory.

Dalai Lama: Did the parish agree with Fred's progressive ministry?

Bill: I'm not sure that they knew. I'm not sure even sure if all of the other priests in the house knew the extent of his hospitality. I never saw the back door locked. I don't think there was a key to it in those days.

Dalai Lama: Did you make friends with anyone who was passing through?

Bill: Language was a problem. Fred was proficient in Spanish and would translate for me when he was able. Other times, it was a matter of signs and gestures. But I could see in the carved, lined faces that horrific events were happening in the world that I could only read about, but not truly understand.

Dalai Lama: Now I see why Fred was your mentor.

Bill: He was my mentor not just because he accepted all people without distinction. He accepted me without conditions as well. The same steak he might prepare for Bishop John McGann he would prepare for any homeless wanderer passing through. I learned not only that all people are to be treated with respect and dignity, but I learned that a true Christian acts ... and only talks about his or her beliefs when necessary.

Dalai Lama: Did you work for Fred?

Bill: I did. I painted for him. His life was meaningful. His example gave me the impetus to continue pursuing my own dream. After twelve years of study, I was ordained a Catholic priest. I was twenty-six years of age.

Dalai Lama: Congratulations! What did you believe that your ordination was about?

Bill: Ordination was a call to service. By accepting this call, I allowed myself to be blessed, broken, taken, and distributed to the people to promote the Kingdom of God. I thought that this was the most meaningful, radical way I could live my life.

Dalai Lama: What does that mean, to offer oneself to be "blessed and broken?"

Bill: For Catholics, the Second Vatican Council gave guidelines on how to be "Eucharist" in the modern world.

Dalai Lama: When was the Vatican Council?

Bill: 1962-1965.

Dalai Lama: And what happened at the Vatican Council?

Bill: All the bishops of the world got together to reflect upon how the people of God were called to live the Gospel in the modern world. They created sixteen documents in all. *Gaudium et Spes,* the Council's document on "The Church in the Modern World," laid out the challenge of Catholic action.

Dalai Lama: Help me with the Latin. What does *Gaudium et Spes* mean?

Bill: *Gaudium et Spes* are the first words of the "Pastoral Constitution on the Church in the Modern World." The bishops declared in the first paragraph that "the joys and the hopes, the griefs and anxieties of the people of this age, especially those who are poor or in any way afflicted—these too are the joys and hopes, the griefs and anxieties of the followers of Christ."

Dalai Lama: In other words, the bishops are saying that they are in solidarity with all humankind.

Bill: That's right.

Dalai Lama: I imagine that this was a shock to the people of the church.

Bill: Well, for those who read it and thought about practicing it, maybe.

Dalai Lama: Bill, pardon my ignorance here, but I have a stereotype of things Catholic. I sometimes think about the church as serving the poor while at the same time serving the wealthy and benefiting from this service.

Bill: That is fair to say.

Dalai Lama: Did people rebel against this newly declared solidarity with all humankind, and in particular, the call to unite with those who are oppressed?

Bill: Not in my experience in the United States, Dalai Lama. The arguments I remember were about whether the mass should remain in Latin or be celebrated in English. The altars were turned around. This created some stir. In the seminary, we had some serious discussion as to whether seminarians should be obligated to attend daily Eucharist.

Dalai Lama: There's that word *Eucharist* again…

Bill: Eucharist is the mass. For Catholic Christians, the resurrected Christ is present in this communal celebration. The bishops at the Council emphasized that the Eucharist is the center of all pastoral activity.

Dalai Lama: You sound like you really knew what you were about.

Bill: I had a lot of energy. I quickly noticed that the ideal for priestly living and the reality often did not match.

Dalai Lama: Do you mean that the job you got was not the job you thought you were going to get?

Bill: Something like that. The parish I was assigned to was the largest on Long Island at that time. There were thirteen thousand registered households. Each time Sunday mass was celebrated, there were no less than one thousand people present.

Dalai Lama: That's a lot of people to be speaking to at one time.

Bill: On my first night in the parish, I was offering prayers at the wake service at the funeral home. A twelve-year-old girl named Maryann Connolly had died of meningitis.

Dalai Lama: Other than your dad, had you experienced death before?

Bill: Other than my dad, no.

Dalai Lama: How did you do?

Bill: Terrible. I had never worn clerical garb in public before this night. I looked into the faces of the grieving parents, and I had no words to say.

Dalai Lama: Maybe your silence was just what was needed.

Bill: Perhaps so. Maryann Connolly's mom and dad later invited me to visit with them. Little did I know that a great ministry awaited them.

Dalai Lama: In what way?

Bill: In a parish that large, there were many deaths of young people. Children died from Sudden Infant Death Syndrome, accidents, sickness, and even suicide. And the Connollys were always there. We started a group called the "Bereaved Parents of St. Joseph."

Dalai Lama: Grieving persons could experience solace and solidarity with others in the same boat. Good idea.

Bill: That was an important experience for me. It made me realize that life gives me experiences that enable me to help people in unique ways.

Dalai Lama: Were you supported in your thinking? I know that, as institutions go, there is a temptation to leave power and control in the hands of management.

Bill: Yes, I felt supported … and encouraged. I had another good mentor at this time of my life.

Dalai Lama: Yes? Who?

Bill: My mentor was a man named Charles Kohli. Have you heard of him?

Dalai Lama: No.

Bill: Do you remember meeting Thomas Merton back in 1968?

Dalai Lama: Ah, yes, I do. Thomas Merton was a Trappist monk. He saw all monasticism as connected—that our different traditions, east and west, all aimed and bringing us to a common awakening.

Bill: Then I must introduce you to Charley Kohli.

Dalai Lama: Sounds interesting.

Bill: It was 1983. Charley Kohli was the eccentric pastor at St. Joseph's Church in Lake Ronkonkoma, on Long Island, New York. Charley and I were watching the news, as we did each evening. Pope John Paul II was conducting a pastoral visitation in Nicaragua. As the Pope was celebrating mass, there were people in the congregation with placards. These women were the "Mothers of the Disappeared." The women shouted some common message to the Pope regarding their missing children. The Pope turned his attention to them. Taking the microphone in hand, he shouted "Silence!" This seemed to make the women shout all the more.

Dalai Lama: And this moved you?

Bill: It did not move me until I saw Charley Kohli jump out of his chair. "What is the Pope doing?" he shouted.

I, in my own New York manner, repeated his questions with a question myself: "Doing? Doing what?"

Charley veered off into a diatribe. "Doesn't the Pope understand that these people have been oppressed under Somoza all these years? Does he know that Somoza is America's man in Central America? Can't he celebrate the fact that the people got together and threw him out? The United States is waging a war against the people of Nicaragua because they are fighting injustice and seeking self-determination."

Dalai Lama: Charley expounded on the connection between religion and politics.

Bill: Yes, but at that moment, I realized that there is no way *not* to play politics.

Dalai Lama: What do you mean?

Bill: That my work as a priest, hearing confessions, burying the dead, comforting the grieving … all this *could* put people to sleep instead of waking them up for some renewed commitment to others. Sure, there is comfort in knowing that there is life after death. But if we do not identify and resist the unhealthy collusion between religion and politics, then we as church can be complicit in evildoing.

Dalai Lama: Bill, from what you said earlier, I thought you were aware of the plight of immigrants, of the effects of the policies of our government on the people of the western hemisphere.

Bill: I was knowledgeable, but at the same time, I was concerned that addressing both politics and religion would alienate the people of my parish. Dalai Lama, I wanted to please everybody. I wanted people to like me. And I may have compromised the Gospel message for fear of rejection.

Dalai Lama: So Charley Kohli's passionate response to a shouting Pope was your "ah-ha" moment?

Bill: What followed that was all part of my own evolution.

Dalai Lama: What happened next?

Bill: Ronald Reagan, who was then President in the United States, decided to ratchet up the arms race and essentially spend the Russians into the poorhouse. He vamped up nuclear arsenals, and, for the first time, began placing them on German soil.

The Second Vatican Council stated: "The arms race is an utterly treacherous trap for humanity, and one which injures the poor to an intolerable degree." St. Joseph's Parish formed a justice and peace community, comprised of conservatives, liberals, Viet Nam veterans, gays and straights, men and women, anti-abortion and anti-nuclear activists. We spoke of the "seamless garment" uniting all life issues. We stood for the sanctity of human life "from the womb to the tomb."

On several occasions, we prayed at sites where life issues were in play. In an effort to hear God's invitation to choose life and stand with those without voice, we fasted, prayed, visited congressional representatives, engaged in civil disobedience, and attempted to live the Eucharist in the world. These were important events on my journey.

Dalai Lama: And Charley Kohli?

Bill: Charley encouraged me all the way. Even John McGann, the bishop who ordained me, publicly chided me but privately encouraged me.

Dalai Lama: How did your bishop chide you publicly and support you privately?

Bill: Charley and I, with the support of our justice and peace community, declared St. Joseph's Church to be a "sanctuary" to Central Americans fleeing the violence of their homelands. The sanctuary concept was a religious and political movement aimed at helping

Central American refugees by sheltering them from the United States Immigration and Naturalization Service authorities. While several other Protestant churches had previously done this, we were the only Catholic church to do so.

Dalai Lama: Did you have Bishop McGann's approval?

Bill: No. When Bishop McGann heard that we declared St. Joseph's a sanctuary, he demanded to see me. Forgoing the traditional clerical garb, I wore a white shirt and black tie to the meeting. I entered his office. He sat behind his desk. He was all business. "Why are you wearing a tie instead of a collar?" he began with notable agitation.

"Bishop," I said, searching for words. "The priest is a call to the community about what the community should be. The clerical clothing is a sign of that call. My life as a priest is a comfortable one. I live much better than most of the people I serve. I am not sure what example I give with my lifestyle. So for that reason, I wear a tie instead of…"

Bishop McGann raised his hand, indicating that he heard enough: "Next time, a clerical collar!"

"Yes, bishop," I answered.

"Now," he said, folding his hands and tapping the desk, kinesthetically moving the conversation from one topic to another, "why have you and Kohli publicly declared St. Joseph's Church a 'sanctuary'?"

"Bishop," I began again, like a runner returning to the starting blocks following a false start, "The Immigration and Naturalization Service is arresting and deporting people from Central America. Even though the enforcement agents' religion does not matter, many of them are Catholic. Once deported, these immigrants face war and death. If we do not…"

Once more, the bishop raised his hand. I took this to mean that he knew about the situation.

"Bill, do you and Charley realize that you are involving yourselves in politics by declaring St. Joseph's parish a sanctuary? You are illegally interfering with the Immigration and Naturalization Service. Do you understand that you endanger the church's tax-exempt status when you do this?"

"But Bishop," I began.

Once again, he raised his hand and continued: "Of course, you must help refugees. You must see Christ in them and help them in any way that one can. But do it quietly. No fanfare. No public declarations. Do you understand?"

"Yes, Bishop," I answered.

"Do not place our tax-exempt status in jeopardy! You understand that we must stay out of politics." The bishop reached across the desk and shook my hand. There was a hint of an unwilling smile on his face. He looked me square in the eye. "And next time," he said, lowering his voice, "Shine your shoes."

I stood and left.

Dalai Lama: Was it a smile on his face or a nervous tic?

Bill: No, it was a smile.

Dalai Lama: Schaefer, Kohli, and McGann were all good and positive mentors.

Bill: And then along came the Maryknoll Fathers and Brothers....

In those days, a recruiter for Maryknoll Brothers called upon me. His name was Del Goodman. He challenged me to volunteer for the missions. The Maryknoll order is a U.S. Catholic overseas mission group. Bishop McGann gave me his blessing. After learning Spanish in Bolivia, I was assigned to the Central American region. I served in Nicaragua, Guatemala, and Honduras. My final destination was El Salvador. Here, my adventure took a new turn.

Dalai Lama: Now this is getting interesting. Bill, what I encourage you to do is to share the story without thinking too much about it. Just as religion can be an obstacle to self-realization and awareness of a oneness with God that already exists before we ask the questions, so can thought and reason derail the insight into truth. With experience, there is healing in the telling.

Bill: I have been in many Latin America countries, but I found something in El Salvador that changed me forever. I arrived to El Salvador on TACA Airlines. It was a warm December afternoon. I looked out the window as the plane soared high over lush, green volcanoes. I saw deep, rich valleys where smoke from wood-burning fires drifted lazily upwards. The plane crossed the tiny country in less than thirty minutes. After a short jaunt over the Pacific Ocean, we turned about and made the descent towards the Comalapa Airport.

Father Fabian Amaya waited for me to pass through customs. The day was swelteringly hot. Soldiers and police dressed in green and black uniforms stood all about the airport.

We drove towards a suburb known as Ilopongo. The streets of the capital, San Salvador, were alive with humanity on the move. Cars picked their way through a sea of people on foot. Ancient, brightly painted busses spewed black exhaust fumes. Fare collectors hung from the open rear doors of these rickety people-movers. Wooden carts drawn by oxen competed with automobiles, bicycles, and pedestrians. It was a study in contrasts, colors, and movement.

Fabian was the first of many generous and committed people that I met in El Salvador. We arrived at his parish house. A meal was laid out before us. I sat at a table with church workers and staff.

"Are you from the United States?" the thin women with high cheekbones politely asked.

"Yes," I answered. "We are here to see how we can support the work of the Basic Christian Communities," I added.

As I spoke, I noticed that all attention drifted towards the television. The scratchy image of a well-groomed, middle-aged man appeared on the screen. I later learned that this was the founder of the ARENA party. His name was Roberto D'Aubisson. All those who watched grimaced as he spoke. The cook gestured to me with pursed eyebrows. The man appeared to anger her. I did not know why. I stood to carry my plate to the sink. The stout, grey-haired cook sidled up to me.

"He's the one who did it," she whispered.

I gave her a questioning look. "The one who did *what?*" I asked.

"He is the one who killed Monseñor Romero."

Dalai Lama: Ah, Monseñor Romero once more.

Bill: Yes, Monseñor Oscar Romero, the assassinated bishop of San Salvador. He was a friend and colleague to my host, Fabian Amaya.

Dalai Lama: How were you going to fit into El Salvador, Bill?

Bill: As a Maryknoll missioner, I was to work with the Salvadoran church to help spread the Kingdom of God.

Dalai Lama: Tell me about the Maryknoll Order.

Bill: Maryknoll is the missionary arm of the church in the United States. Maryknoll had worked in El Salvador since the 1950s. After elections were overturned by the military in 1972 and 1977, the country descended into civil war. In March, 1980, Monseñor Oscar Romero was murdered. On December 2nd of that year, two Maryknoll sisters, an Ursuline sister, and a lay colleague were raped and murdered after they drove from the airport in San Salvador. The United States took the position that the war was the result of foreign intervention by Cuba and the Soviet Union and placed its might with the military. President José Napoleón Duarte, who studied at Notre Dame and founded the Boy Scouts in El Salvador, told the Maryknoll authorities that he could no longer promise protection to American missionaries working in the country.

As the civil war ground on in El Salvador, the Maryknoll Order pulled out of the country. There was a desire to return to the country later and continue the work of the church. The official pastoral plan of the church was described as a "preferential option for the poor." The newspapers and military generally saw priests and church workers as subversives, communists, and potential terrorists. I was a member of the return team.

Dalai Lama: What does the Spanish term rendered into English as "accompanying the people" mean?

Bill: "Accompanying the people" means living with the people and experiencing reality from their point of view. It begins with the belief in the incarnation. Since Christ became human, all human life reflects the divine. The church in Latin America declared that while Christ is present in every human being, there is a unique challenge to see and love Christ in those who are poor and oppressed. This led to many anguished conversations about commitment. The question was posed like this: how did the lifestyle of all Christians, but especially priests and nuns, reflect a commitment to Christ in the poor? How did celibate ministers and Christians show faithful solidarity with those without power and without voice?

In El Salvador, as in most Latin American countries, ninety per cent of the resources were vested in the hands of ten percent of the population. The vast majority of persons were both very young and very poor. A tiny percentage of people were wealthy and formed the oligarchy. The same Gospel was read in the upscale Escalón neighborhood as in the poorer communities like Soyapongo and Zacamíl. Reflections on that same Gospel took Christians in different directions depending on the neighborhoods where they lived and the basic Christian communities to which they belonged.

To protect their perceived interests, some of the wealthy and their hires joined death squads. Men dressed in civilian clothes made nighttime raids on poor communities like Zacamíl. They woke up households in the middle of the night. They seized persons suspected of being subversives or terrorists from their beds. In the morning—if they were fortunate—their bodies turned up on roadsides or in the piled-high garbage that lined the streets of San Salvador. Sometimes, the body of a loved one was discovered weeks or months after having "been disappeared." Often, the bodies were never found at all.

This fueled an urgency to read the Gospel from the perspective of that present reality. "What does God invite us to do in the midst of injustice, given that we have dignity and worth?" For some, it meant

59

joining the forces of resistance that sought to counter the "official" violence of the U.S.-supported government. For others, it meant waiting on God to intervene. So it was into this mix that I was stepping. If one enjoys adventures, I picked a good one.

Dalai Lama: Is this what is meant by Liberation Theology?

Bill: Yes, this was Liberation Theology. It means hearing and applying the message of sacred scripture in a given place and time.

I was assigned to El Salvador with two Maryknoll veterans who would know how to best roll with the shifting, precarious situation.

John Halbert was a member of the Maryknoll Provincial Council. He was a white-haired academic in his mid-fifties. He had plenty of experience in the classroom, but not a whole lot of experience in mission. He was organized, slightly cynical, and driven.

Ron Hennessey had spent more than thirty years working in Central America. He was a veteran of the United States Army. During the Korean War, he served as a sergeant in the motor pool. Both were ordained priests before or during the Vatican Council. Ron worked mostly with the indigenous population in Guatemala. After many years of ministry in Guatemala's Petén region, he moved to the Guatemalan highlands. During the years he was there, there was a systemic effort to exterminate the Indian population. I first met Ron in San Mateo Ixtatán. I can still see the lined, weathered face of this stoic son of Iowan farmers tear up as he described a massacre he witnessed in San Mateo Ixtatán.

Dalai Lama: I cannot think of better men to be serving with in the new venture into El Salvador.

Bill: I arrived to El Salvador ahead of both Halbert and Hennessey. I carried a message for Archbishop Arturo Rivera y Damas from my Maryknoll superior, Bill Mullan: "As Maryknollers, we are going to take six months before accepting an assignment."

Dalai Lama: I imagine they had immediate needs and work for you to do as soon as you arrived.

Bill: You are right. The day after I arrived, I was informed of an appointment at the offices in the Diocese of San Salvador. The meeting was with Archbishop Rivera y Damas and Monseñor Ricardo Urioste, the vicar general of the Archdiocese of San Salvador.

In the parking lot at the chancery, Father Fabian Amaya emerged from the car. Barefoot women with long, worn aprons greeted him with broad smiles. The killing of priests was in fashion in San Salvador. One shadowy group, the White Warrior League, placed posters on utility poles that read: "Be a patriot! Kill a priest." Priests suffered the same fate as the people they served.

Pio was the name of Fabian's driver. He walked behind Fabian like some dedicated secret service agent. He looked as if he were expecting trouble. He appeared ready to protect Fabian as circumstances mandated. He moved with Fabian past the people standing in the parking lot waiting to gain entry into to the office of 'Tutela Legal," the Salvadoran Church's human rights arm. I followed behind the two men.

The chancery building was not like any typical church office in the United States. The weathered walls sported peeling yellow paint. The concrete floor was worn and cracked. Neatly-dressed workers nodded their heads and stepped aside as Fabian passed. There was a sense of triumph and unity between Fabian and the workers, perhaps a sense that they had all survived another day. Fabian greeted the people with genuine interest. In return, they showed him respect. In such times, they took nothing for granted.

Fabian mounted the stairs leading to the second floor. We arrived at the Archbishop's office. The door was ajar. Fabian gave a subdued knock. The voice of the Archbishop rang out. *"Pasan adelante,"* he called out. "Step inside."

Fabian entered the room. Pio and I entered behind him. Pio took his place in a far corner. I stood in the middle of the room. Fabian and Archbishop Rivera y Damas shook hands. The Archbishop wore a long, black cassock. His forehead and face were deeply lined, especially around his eyes. His hair was thinning and slicked back. Fabian presented me to Urioste and Rivera y Damas.

"This is Padre Guillermo from Maryknoll," Fabian said with an expansive gesture in my direction. Archbishop Rivera y Damas moved towards me. "Welcome to El Salvador," he said, pumping my hand with a strong, enthusiastic handshake. Ricardo Urioste stepped forward. He wore a black clerical suit. His jacket was buttoned. His white collar seemed to shine. He appeared to be in his early sixties. He spoke both English and Spanish deliberately, choosing his words with care. His expression was subdued as if many disparate thoughts crowded his mind. Fabian's green, close-fitting dress shirt called a *guayabera* contrasted with the black clerical garb worn by his colleagues. His smile revealed a lifelong gap between his front teeth. His large, black glasses rode high upon the bridge of his nose. His olive-colored skin and black hair recalled his indigenous roots.

"We are very glad that you are here," Archbishop Rivera y Damas began. "Please be seated."

I took my place in a chair near his desk. "We are having difficulty filling one parish assignment. We hope that you and your Maryknoll congregation might help us here. The name of the sector is Zacamíl." Archbishop Rivera y Damas studied my face to sense my reaction to his proposal. He wondered aloud, "Have you heard of this place before?"

Dalai Lama: I also wondered if you saw this coming.

Bill: No, Dalai Lama. I had not heard of this place before. But what he shared made me curious. I realized that they were hoping to send us to a parish where the people felt forced to flee and fight.

Fabian continued: "Fathers Pedro and Rogelio served in Zacamíl. They have left the parish and gone to the eastern department of Morazán. This is where the guerrilla group, the Revolutionary Army of the People, is the strongest. Before these Belgian priests, Salvadoran

Fathers Octavio Ortiz and Edgar Palacios were pastors in Zacamíl. Both were killed."

As I listened, I heard a distant explosion. *Booooom!* I could feel a vibration from the explosion through the concrete floor of Archbishop Rivera y Damas' office. The three clerics noted my distraction by the not-so-distant rumble. Rivera y Damas offered an awkward smile: "That sound you hear comes from a volcano called Guazapa. It is twenty kilometers from San Salvador. The army bombs the area day and night in an effort to drive out the rebels." Archbishop Rivera y Damas paused with appreciation for the silence: "The area of Zacamíl is not without priests," he said. "The Jesuits at the Central American University are working in Zacamíl until we can find replacements. Ignacio Ellacuría, Amando Lopez, Jose María Tojeira and Joaquín Baró are there now. They will help you to make the transition."

"We wish to wait six months prior to taking a parish," I informed Fabian. The rotund Fabian quietly listened.

The Archbishop asked, "Would you like to see Zacamíl?"

"Sure," I said.

Fabian shook hands with Archbishop Rivera y Damas and Ricardo Urioste. Pio nodded from his place by the door. I shook hands with both men. Off we went.

Dalai Lama: In such places, wonderful things are to be found.

Bill: We drove north from the diocesan offices. Once more, the driver, Pio, wove his way through crowds of people walking the street. Since there was bombing and efforts to eradicate the insurgency in the countryside, twenty percent of the population—some one million people—had been displaced from the rural areas to the capital city of San Salvador and beyond.

We moved slowly north towards the National University. The sun-baked, weathered yellow walls were still pock-marked from bullets and explosives. We drove the perimeter of the university as Pio competed with buses jammed with travelers. Winding about the university complex, we arrived at the only traffic light in Zacamíl. At the stoplight, we sat in the middle of a veritable sea of apartment buildings. To the right, thousands of apartment dwellers lived in a community known collectively as *el Hoyo*. To the left, thousands more people made their homes in four-story, grey and white cinderblock apartment buildings in a community bearing the name *Ayuda Mutua*, or Mutual Aid. In between and around the apartments buildings, soccer fields and green space provided living space to refugees and the displaced. Makeshift shacks of cardboard and tin dotted the landscape. These provisional, threadbare communities bore the names like San Sebastian, Divine Providence, and Emmanuel, a name meaning "God is with us." After a series of right turns, we arrived in a residential area known as Yanira. There, in the middle of the block, stood a non-descript, grey, cinderblock structure. "Here it is," announced Fabian. "This is the parish church of Cristo Salvador."

The sun was high in the sky as Pio, Fabian, and I emerged on the narrow street. Fabian had the same watchful look as he moved towards the square building. We climbed the three smooth, concrete steps to a large, red, sheet-metal door. Fabian's knock on the door resonated in what seemed an empty expanse inside. A second knock, and footprints could be heard approaching from inside. With a loud creak, the door swung open towards us. There stood a light-skinned, middle-aged man.

Dalai Lama: Was he the custodian?

Bill: No. The man's name was Martín Baro. Everyone called him "Nacho." He was the head of the psychology department at the Central American University José Simeon Cañas. I sensed his unease when he opened that big door. He seemed surprised to find us standing there. He looked at Fabian with uncertainty.

"Hello, Nacho," smiled Fabian, offering a handshake to the balding professor. Fabian turned to me. "This is Guillermo. He is new to El Salvador. Do you have time to sit?"

"Come," Nacho said. As the door opened wide, a circle of women came into view. They sat on metal chairs on the tile floor. "Come, meet some of these women," Nacho said, motioning towards the circle. Nacho's accent suggested that he was from Spain.

The women were dressed in black. With a grand gesture, Nacho introduced us. "You all know Padre Fabian Amaya," he said with the hint of cynicism. The women nodded warily. "This is Guillermo. He is visiting San Salvador." This time, there was little acknowledgment. I read more suspicion than welcome.

A thin woman with a white kerchief atop her head asked, "Are you from the United States?"

"Yes," I answered. "I am from the United States."

Father Nacho smiled at the women and asked, "Who would like to tell Guillermo about why we are here?"

A woman in her forties looked down at her folded hands, gathered her thoughts, and began: "We are the 'Mothers of the Disappeared.' Each woman you see here has a story. I can only tell one … mine." A respectful silence filled the room. "My son was not a member of any political group. He belonged to a parish youth group here in Zacamíl. He was on a retreat with Father Octavio Ortiz in a neighborhood called San Antonio Abad. In the middle of the retreat, tanks rolled into the compound. Soldiers surrounded the retreat house. My son 'disappeared' after that. The newspapers reported that the retreat was really a political meeting. It said that the church youth groups were urban guerrillas in disguise. I do not believe that."

A loud silence ensued. The tall, thin woman with striking facial features leaned forward. Her chin rested on the palms of her hands. She pondered some distant point in her mind. Suddenly, this second woman stood to speak. "In my case," she began, "My husband and I argued about leaving the Catholic Church. He felt that it was too risky for our family. The newspapers constantly wrote that the 'Basic Christian Community' movement promotes Communism. They say that Fidel Castro is behind the activism of the university students and the church's 'preferential option for the poor.' Because my faith is strong, I did not want to look for another church. Before we could make a decision, that's when it happened."

"What happened?" I asked. I gazed over at Nacho. He sat quietly listening. His head was tilted downwards, his bearded chin resting on the palm of his right hand.

"It was a cool morning," she began. "We had no eggs in the house. I sent my boy to the market behind the place where the bus number twenty-three stops. He had to cross the street that runs through the center of Zacamíl. A white jeep with polarized windows was parked up the hill. As he stepped off the sidewalk, a car raced towards him. A woman near the bus stop told me that she saw two men dressed in civilian clothes running after him. They apprehended him about a block from the traffic light. The men wrestled him into a Jeep Cherokee. I was frantic. For over a week, I looked for him at the offices of all the security and police offices. I even went to see if National Guard had him. Everyone I spoke to said they knew nothing about his whereabouts."

As she spoke, the lined faces of the women grew deeper as the tale unfolded. This was their therapy time with Nacho. Their slight nods of understanding provided the support needed for their healing.

"Early one Tuesday morning, a neighbor came to my house. 'There are bodies dumped in the garbage on the street,' she said. I ran as quickly as my legs could carry me. I reached the curbside where the garbage was piled high. I hoped that, if my son were dead, that I might find his body. 'If he is dead,' I thought, 'at least he will not be suffering.' As I walked north towards the Yanira neighborhood, I scanned the plastic milk bottles, burlap bags, and husks of corn for some part of a human body. I noticed that people were passing by something that slowed their pace. I wondered what they were looking at. My heart leapt. There was a body face up in the trash. It was the body of a dead young man. The body was wrapped in some pink packing paper. The man had a sign tied about his neck. It read, 'Subversive.' It was my son. I could not recover his body. My whole family would have been targeted by the death squads. I said a small prayer. I thanked God that at least I knew where he was. I told myself that he was at peace."

"There was nothing more that you could have done, "Nacho reassured her. "You have other children at home. Had you claimed his body, they may have taken you as well as your other children."

We listened silently to several other stories. Father Nacho invited all to stand and pray the Lord's Prayer, and then the meeting concluded.

Dalai Lama: Were you ready for such a "meet and greet" type of experience, Bill?

Bill: No, Dalai Lama. I was not ready. I could not conceive that people were being killed because of an alignment between faith and politics. I knew about the "preferential option for the poor," but I never imagined the implications for living the Gospel with such an option. While the North American Church tried to embrace the documents of Vatican II and turned the altars around, this Church of Latin America had taken those same documents and read something totally different. Eventually, they stated that being faithful to the Gospel meant standing with the poor.

Dalai Lama: On paper, this seems obvious. If you believe that God took on human form in Christ, then all humans are, in some way, Christ or God. So did you take the assignment to work in Zacamíl?

Bill: Yes.

Dalai Lama: What did you learn there?

Bill: I learned that there is such a thing as being above politics. If I say that I am not political, then I promote the status quo. I also learned that friendship and love are stronger than hatred and death.

Dalai Lama: So how did you manage?

Bill: Thanks to the friendship of Ron Hennessey, and the people of Zacamìl, I laughed a lot and grew each day.

Dalai Lama: What was it about Ron that helped you so?

Bill: In the war years in El Salvador, I came to know Ron as if he were an elder brother. Ron was born during the Depression years. He was the eleventh of fifteen children. He grew up in Ryan, Iowa, where he worked on the family farm. We prayed the "Liturgy of the Hours" each morning and each evening. We went to army bases to intervene for families whose sons were forcibly recruited. We tried to show by our actions that we saw Christ in every person, both young and old. It did not matter if they were guerrillas fighting against the government or soldiers fighting for the government. If they had to hide from death squads, we helped them hide. If a judge was threatened because he sought justice, we supported him. If people were displaced from the countryside to the city, we tried to find ways to get them connected, to get them the basic necessities of survival.

It was with death of Herbert Anaya that not even Ron's friendship was helpful to keep me emotionally afloat.

Dalai Lama: Who was Herbert Anaya?

Bill: Herbert Anaya was the head of the Non-Governmental Human Rights office. He lived in our community in Zacamíl. On the morning of October 26, 1987, he was leaving his house to take two of his five children to school. As he approached his car, he was murdered in the parking lot in front of his house.

Dalai Lama: Did you have anything to do with him?

Bill: I received a call to officiate at a mass for him at the cathedral. The only problem was that the cathedral had once more been occupied by the guerrillas of the FMLN. A group of neighbors and parishioners from Zacamíl carried Herbert's body to the cathedral in downtown San Salvador. It was dark. The crowd carrying his body grew as we walked towards the center of the city. By the time the crowd walked past the U.S. Embassy, it grew to about two hundred people. It was impossible to see the faces of most of the marchers. As the people walked, they chanted: "Yankee Invader, get out of El Salvador." This did place me in an awkward position. After all, I was from New York, home of the Yankees ... baseball, that is. When we passed under lights near the embassy, I heard my name being mentioned. People were saying, "Guillermo is here," or something to this effect.

Dalai Lama: Were you in the wrong place at the wrong time?

Bill: Well, a marcher sidled up to me. He had a red bandana covering his face. "Hey, Guillermo," he said, "When we say 'Yankee Invader,' do not take it personally."

Dalai Lama: That is unusual. So what did you do?

Bill: I smiled and kept walking towards the cathedral.

Dalai Lama: Where was Archbishop Rivera y Damas in all of this?

Bill: Archbishop Rivera y Damas, who succeeded Archbishop Romero, tried hard to keep the gospel message front and center. The day we carried Herbert Anaya's body to the cathedral, he called me up. "Guillermo," he said to me.

"Yes, Archbishop?" I responded.

"I understand that you were asked to celebrate the mass for Herbert Anaya."

"Yes, that is true," I answered.

"That is good. Celebrate the mass. But tell the guerrillas inside the cathedral that this is the eighteenth time the cathedral has been occupied. Tell them that I want this to be the last time."

"Yes, Archbishop," I replied.

Dalai Lama: That is scary stuff.

Bill: When we got to the cathedral, militants were shouting slogans into megaphones. As I entered the building, I was searched for weapons. Strangely enough, the man who searched me had a son in our community. The boy was somehow later charged with Herbert Anaya's murder.

Dalai Lama: What did it look like inside the cathedral?

Bill: I first saw two of Herbert's small children. They sat next to their father's body. Herbert's coffin lay atop some folded chairs in the center of the cavernous, half-completed structure. Monseñor Modesto Lopez, rector of the cathedral, sent some wine and hosts so that mass could be celebrated. Denunciations of the U.S. government and President Ronald Reagan could be heard echoing in the plaza outside the church. I found a place to sit and waited for mass to begin.

Dalai Lama: Where did you sit?

Bill: Most cathedrals are built in the shape of a cross. On the right side of the cathedral, the body of Monseñor Oscár Romero lay in state. I often enjoyed sitting here on my days off. One could hardly describe Romero's tomb as sad. Much human activity was going on around the place the day that Archbishop Romero was buried. Country folk would picnic there and visit with one another. Children would color and hang their pictures on the walls. So, too, on this day, upon entering the cathedral, I sat near the body of Oscár Romero. Since a state of siege was in force, I needed to catch a bus home before six o'clock p.m. or risk being shot. "Can we begin the mass?" I called out, my voice echoing across the voluminous space. The shouting of anti-American sentiments stopped. The upper and lower door and windows to the cathedral closed. Armed men and women approached the center of the cathedral. One of the guerrillas opened a hymnal. She asked all to turn to the song entitled in Spanish, "Love is to Give of Oneself." The small but spirited band of rebel mourners sang all the verses to the song:

"To love is to give of oneself,

To search for what might make others happy.

To love is to give of oneself."

Dalai Lama: I can see your dilemma: armed men and women who sing that their commitment to love means dying for a political cause.

Bill: I never understood how people could fight oppression with violence. Then again, my faith or other life experiences did not prepare me for the complexities of living in a place like El Salvador. On Long

Island, the world normally fits together nicely. If I avoided sin and loved others, then I would go to heaven. In prior years, on Saturday nights, I would wait in line outside the velvet-curtained confessional. When my turn came, I would enter the dark box and kneel before a perforated, metal screen. As a little door slid open, the profile of a man in shadow became visible. I poured forth my sins: fighting with my brothers and sisters; cursing; disobeying my parents; and so forth. I received penance and absolution, and when I left, I felt forgiven

Dalai Lama: And if death caught you off guard, you were ready for life everlasting?

Bill: That's the bottom line.

Dalai Lama: Is that an aspect of Liberation Theology?

Bill: There is a kind of liberation that happens with that world view. Chaos is the product of sin and is temporary. All sin can be pardoned. But as I looked at Herbert's poor body and his weeping family, the naiveté of my world view weighed upon me. I wanted greater clarity. I wanted to see Christians and churches live up to the ideals about which they preached.

Dalai Lama: No church, no mosque, no temple, no organization lives up to the ideals that their founders put forth. You wanted perfect clarity and altruism. You were offended by men and women taking up arms in the name of Christ and the Gospel. You were also frustrated with yourself and your North American church and government.

Bill: I knew how to say "yes" to life in the face of death, but not in a geopolitical context where a minority of wealthy Christians held sway over the resources and governance of the masses. Nowadays, the saying is "follow the money." I never believed this was true of church matters, but it was.

Dalai Lama: So, then, what happened?

Bill: We celebrated mass for Herbert Anaya. With the permission of government authorities, we were later able to take his body from the cathedral and give him a proper burial.

Dalai Lama: Were the people of Long Island interested in Herbert Anaya and many like him that you came to know?

Bill: When I attempted to return to the United States, I found it impossible to return home again. In the 1980s, a man named William Casey was head of the Central Intelligence Agency. He was a staunch, conservative Catholic living in Roslyn Harbor, Long Island. He was a key player in arming the Nicaraguan Contras. He masterminded the selling of weapons to Iran, which, at the time, was designated a terrorist state, in order to produce hard cash to generate funds used to create, train, and arm soldiers attacking the new Sandinista regime in Nicaragua. This all took place under the watch of John Negroponte, then ambassador to Honduras, and later the first head of Homeland Security. Bill Casey had the resistant ear of John McGann, Bishop of Rockville Centre.

As the Berlin Wall came down in 1989 and demonstrators stood up to the government in China at Tiananmen Square, a so-called "final offensive" took place in El Salvador. Father Armando and his fellow Jesuits on the faculty at the Catholic University were killed during this final offensive by troops armed and trained by my own government at the "School of the Americas" at Fort Benning, Georgia. One month before the offensive, in October, 1989, I was invited by the director of the diocesan Society for the Propagation of the Faith, Monsignor Lawrence Ballweg, to return to Long Island to speak at a mass celebrated at the diocesan Cathedral of St. Agnes by Bishop John McGann. Arrangements were made for my travel to the United States and for my stay while on Long Island. The day before I was scheduled to leave El Salvador, I received an urgent message from Monsignor Ballweg stating that my invitation to speak had been withdrawn since "several Jesuits had already spoken at the Cathedral." In lieu of a missionary preacher, a popular Franciscan retreat director and spiritual writer, Father Richard Rohr, was invited to speak at the liturgy.

Dalai Lama: Were you surprised by this?

Bill: I was surprised ... I had planned to use this occasion to consider my re-entry to ministry in New York. I was now identified with a group that some prominent church leaders considered radical and dangerous. That group was the Jesuits. Father Daniel Berrigan, a famous anti-war activist, had preached at the first mass of thanksgiving of a newly-ordained St. Agnes parishioner several years previously. Only days after the withdrawal of my invitation, the Jesuits at the University of Central America in San Salvador were targeted and executed by soldiers armed and trained by the United States.

Dalai Lama: Were the Jesuits promoting violence?

Bill: They were not. They made every effort to practice the "preferential option for the poor," which was the expressed diocesan pastoral plan also articulated by the Latin American bishops at their conferences in Medellín, Colombia, in 1968 and at Puebla, Mexico, in 1979. As a result of preaching the Gospel in that particular place and time, they suffered their fate: the extermination of their lives. On the morning of November 16, 1989, these Jesuit confreres and my brothers lay dead, spread out on the lawn in their blood-splattered pajamas, along with their housekeeper and her daughter. Their blood seeped into the Salvadoran earth in front of their university residence. I was some two miles away, avoiding shelling and aerial strafing with the men, women, and children of the Zacamíl community. The Jesuits and hundreds of Salvadorans paid the ultimate price of apostleship. This is fidelity to the model Christ provides. Their faithfulness was somehow lost to many in the higher echelons of the church. From Rome to the various national conferences of Catholic bishops, many saw the "preferential option for the poor" as watered-down Marxism. With such simple analysis, there was nothing to learn from the church. After their deaths, I lost my ability to find meaning in discrete acts of ministry. I felt that something was wrong with me. How would I be able to let go of memories and betrayals?

Dalai Lama: Bill, it is time to let go of the Jesuits and even your friend, Oscar Romero. It is time to see that what women like Dorothy Kazel, Jean Donovan, Maura Clark, and Ita Ford did was being faithful to their mission on earth. It is now your time to serve and love without counting the cost. It may well mean persecution and misunderstanding. But that is not something I need tell you.

Bill: I am ready to live the best life I know how. I am angered by the refusal to understand the reasons so many people emigrate from their places of origin, from the lands that they cherish. Immigrants are God's gift to America and to other nations in which they reside. Instead of welcome, they are often targeted for reprisals by fearful, ignorant persons both within and outside the churches.

Dalai Lama: One cannot change everyone. One can change one's own self. Recognize God is in the ordinary events and people with whom you come into contact in everyday life.

Bill: Thomas Merton said that he could tell a saint by the way a woman or a man picked up a piece of paper. Is this enough?

Dalai Lama: Bill, begin with attentiveness. Yes. Holiness is attending to the life forces about yourself and within yourself. It is then that you will put love into action with courage. This is the meaning of justice.

Bill: What does it say about me when I am so taken by distraction and fear?

Dalai Lama: This is the human condition. The mind moves from one image, one thought, to another. You must quiet the mind through spiritual practice. You must know your history and your life experience to see where these thoughts come from. You will then see the wisdom of the words, "Fear is useless; what is needed is trust."

Bill: I try to help every person see that his or her life is a great adventure.

Dalai Lama: I understand this from my Buddhist tradition. The cause of all suffering is *Samudaya,* the desire to have or control things.

Bill: I have carried these and many experiences with the hope of learning from them and letting them go. Until I shared them with you, I lived in grief. Now these same experiences can help propel me to health, wisdom, and holiness.

Dalai Lama: Yes, you can share these experiences to heal, to gain wisdom, and to be a healer of your own inner self. You must first free yourself of all desire and possession. The heart of true compassion begins with the desire to possess nothing.

Bill: I often felt that faithfulness meant adherence to a set of external principles and traditions. I factored out my own experience in an effort be faithful to the principles.

Dalai Lama: In the end, one must be faithful to one's own true self. If you are faithful to yourself, you will be faithful to the laws and traditions of your belief system. It is the source of happiness here. It is that by which God judges and humankind benefits.

Bill: May I call upon you at another time?

Dalai Lama: Yes, of course, Bill, anytime.

It is now time to share the reader's own, individual story. Now that the journal keeper has selected his or her imaginary mentor in mind, begin to quiet oneself down. Sit before the chosen mentor. Close your eyes, and in your imagination, see the mentor sitting before you. Notice what he or she looks like: the face, the clothing, and the hands. You will begin each writing session with the same meditation. Begin by quieting yourself. Once you find some quiet time and space, begin to write. Allow your imagination to dictate the conversation.

CHAPTER 7

GROWING UP AS FATHER: THE STORIES OF MARRIED CATHOLIC PRIESTS

It was an overcast December morning in Houston, Texas. Driving south on Highway 59, I fiddled with the volume button on my failing car radio. As the impressive Houston skyline came into view, I heard the news that Cardinal Claude Hummes has proposed the creation of prayer groups to "pray for victims of sexual abuse by priests."

"Is it enough," I wondered, "to pray for the victims without understanding and correcting those mechanisms which made such abuses possible?"

Catholic priests remain in the news.

Father Alberto Cutiè is the handsome face of Roman Catholicism for millions in the Spanish speaking world.

A charismatic Jesuit priest from South Beach, Florida, Father Alberto joins the Episcopal church after photos taken of him and a woman friend surface.

Father Brian McKeon is accused of sexual molestation and defrocked by the acting bishop of Diocese of Rockville Centre, New York. At age fifty nine, he dies a broken man.

The president of Paraguay, Fernando Lugo, is a former Roman Catholic bishop. Shortly after his presidential inauguration, three women come forward claiming that he is the father of their children.

What is going on here?

Former seminary rector and author Bishop Emil Wcela told me of the death of an old professor of mine. Father Julian Miller taught dogma at Immaculate Conception Seminary in the Diocese of Rockville Centre in the 1970s. He resigned from the priesthood and died in 2007. He was alone in his apartment, his phone off the hook. That image of him dying unable to communicate his experience as a resigned priest is a metaphor. The story he had to tell will never be heard

What can we learn from these experiences?

My doctoral dissertation at the University of Houston was titled *The Mid-Life Role Exit of Roman Catholic Priests: A Grounded Theory Study*. Grounded Theory is an inductive research methodology that invites the researcher to drop any prejudices and assumptions and to listen for the meaning persons ascribe to their lives, experiences, and ministries. I did not begin with defined tenets and theories. Instead, I invited these men to share their own journeys. Over time, I came to understand those common themes relating to the experience of "leaving priesthood." I concluded that fidelity can take many forms.

I was ordained a priest on May 17, 1980, by Bishop John McGann. Months after the Final Offensive in El Salvador, I returned to the United States in 1990 and resigned from "active ministry." Bishop McGann placed his hands on my head once again, blessed me, and wished me all the best in my life outside of priesthood. A year later, I married Ana. In a letter dated April 25, 1995, he wrote the following:

Dear Bill,

I am happy to hear that you are enjoying your work—your ministry—in counseling ministers and others in Texas. I am also delighted to hear of the health and happiness of your wife and two children.

We all serve in different capacities and sometimes in various roles during life. I respect your decisions to respond to the Gospel through a variety of ministries. Your promise of respect and obedience to the Lord continues in your work today and in your family life. There is no doubt that you have always been attentive and obedient to the call of God in your life, Bill. I believe as you do that, paradoxically, the decisions you have made are in keeping with the essential promises you expressed.

I wish you success as you begin your doctorate in social work and in all your continuing endeavors to "serve the Lord with gladness."

Fraternally Yours in Christ,
Most Reverend John R. McGann, D.D.
Bishop of Rockville Centre

A vocation to the priesthood in the American Catholic experience was traditionally considered a blessing and privilege to the candidate and to the candidate's family, extending to the priest's ethnic grouping. A dutiful acceptance of a 'felt' calling, a submission of the self to church authorities, the rejection of the world and its standards—these were powerful dynamics in attracting extremely talented sons to the immigrant church. The priest was adulated and was elevated to the stature of an almost mythic respect and dignity in the community.

Religious formation and education in America was significantly structured and contained within it the theological and anthropological belief that the human being is a rational animal composed of the regal power of reason and the unruly powers of passions such as anger and sexuality. The conditions of seminary training included removal from the world, strict discipline, and the reduction of social contacts which arrested, to one degree or another, the development of the seminarians. Intimacy in any form was discouraged. Self-development and pride in self were discouraged, since the future priest was expected to be another Christ by appropriating to himself the doctrine of the Cross. "If a man wishes to come after me, he must deny his very self, take up his cross, and follow in my steps. Whoever would preserve his life will lose it, and whoever loses his life for my sake and the Gospel's will preserve it" (Mark 8:34). The result was that future priests advanced cognitively, but emotionally and psychologically, their development was often arrested.

Leaving the priesthood has always been difficult. Just how difficult depended upon the historical era in which a man resigned. If he withdrew prior to Vatican II, it was assumed that the priest had assumed a mistaken vocation or was incompetent. His withdrawal from the active ministry was hidden from the membership of the church and from society. The resigned priest was considered a "stray shepherd" and was regarded suspiciously by others.

> To attempt to conceal that fact that there are many stray shepherds living in our big cities is unwise …Some are immigrant from other countries. The majority seek to hide away in the mass of people, unknown so far as their past is concerned. Some, however, take up a ministry of preaching in a non-Catholic sect. Some take up a bitter pen to write against the mother they once loved so well. (Shepherds in the Mist, Barret, 1948)

Of the resigned priest, Cardinal Cushing wrote,

> Let us think for a moment of these wandering shepherds bereft of all dignity, lost and alone although they walk in crowds …How pitiful the plight of the fallen priest! How far he has fallen! How terrible his wounds …Of all God's children, does he love least those who once loved Him most?

If his departure occurred during or after the Vatican Council, his departure was now in the open, since thousands of priests withdrew at this time. Resignation from priesthood was now discussed openly. Some priests gave negative reasons for their withdrawal, addressing organizational, theological, and interpersonal factors. Others maintained that a commitment to love motivated them in the direction of role-exit.

Regardless of circumstances or motivations, the experience of role exit from priesthood is traditionally a painful one. The transition from religious to secular life is often traumatic, characterized by psychological feelings of guilt and fear which can render the transition a wrenching and dreadful experience.

Why do some men remain in priesthood while others choose to leave? In addressing these questions, I sent a questionnaire to 450 active and inactive Roman Catholic priests from each of the fifty states. Adapting a survey created by Andrews and Withey entitled *Social Indicators of Well-being: Americans' Perceptions of Life Quality* (1976), I attempted to survey the priest's sense of his own well-being while in active ministry. The survey tapped the man's general feelings regarding his life as a priest, living situation, feelings about himself, present assignment, health, finances, privacy, safety, enjoyment, relationship to family, accomplishment, money, friends, freedom, living standard, psychological well-being, ability to resolve problems, relationship to authority, acceptance by others, dealings with Church authority, and feelings about spare time, manhood, work environment, and celibacy. Other information obtained included years spent as a priest, age, ethnicity, and income. A direct discriminate function statistical analysis was performed to determine and to discriminate between those factors leading a man to exit or remain in ministry.

The loading matrix of correlations between the twenty-eight predictor variables and the discriminate function showed that the primary predictors for resignation were loneliness and the practice of celibacy. The average age of transition from active ministry was 39.4 years.

The National Catholic Conference of Bishops established the Priestly Life and Ministry Committee. This committee has encouraged the establishment of policies, structures, and organizations that have a significant impact on the priests in the United States. In 1988, the committee turned its attention to the morale of priests in the United States.

"Priestly Morale" begins with a call for priests to face the challenges of a new world. It acknowledges that "the American priest is subject to predictable pressures from the lifestyle he has inherited in a changing world and church, especially in the areas of sexuality, authority, and affluence. While he is coping creditably well, he is 'hurting' in some ways." Men are challenged to move from the "rugged individualism that has characterized much of priestly spirituality in the recent past and to return to a spirit of the apostolic life of the primitive church."

Each priest is reminded that he is a servant-leader whose ministry is rooted in the mystery of the risen Lord and the church. "The pastor becomes a religious symbol of tradition, the keeper and speaker of the revealed word in all its rich expressions. He becomes the religious symbol of God's care for his people, expressing compassion for the wounded and outrage at injustice. He becomes the religious symbol of order, calling the community to an effective stewardship of its gifts and shared use of its resources." It is against these religious themes of spirituality, servanthood, and leadership that the Bishops' Committee on Priestly Life addresses the subject of morale.

The bishops suggest that morale is, first and foremost, an internal state of mind with regard to hope and confidence. As such, it is first of all the responsibility of the individual priest. At the same time, the morale of priests has a common context for which church leaders have a mutual responsibility. While recognizing that "there exists today a serious and substantial morale problem among priests in general," the problem cannot be simply attributed to one or another cause or recent event. They name several variables they perceive as linked to the crisis concerning priestly morale.

1. *Role expectations* among clergy leave many feeling trapped, overworked, frustrated, and with a sense of little or no time for themselves. The continuing shortage of clergy is coupled with directives which focus on duties which "only the priest can do." For many priests, there is a lack of a unified, coherent vision of what the role expectations are. The confluence of these factors, coupled with the times in which we live, has led many priests to settle for a part-time presence to their priesthood. Many priests, especially those between the ages of forty-five and sixty-nine, have elected to "drop out quietly." Others have assumed an "I don't do windows" attitude, rejecting traditional job descriptions of "always on duty" or "all things to all people." The committee notes that while such attitudes may reflect a relatively small number of priests, it impacts the attitudes and morale of others. The result is that priests experience a "bone weariness" that comes from standing in the breach during a time of profound cultural and historical transition.

2. The *declining number* of active priests takes its toll on morale from three perspectives: present practice, clouded personal future, and solutions which are precluded from discussion.

With regard to present pastoral practice, the priesthood has always had its share of men limited in energies, skills, and on-the-job presence. In the past, greater numbers of priests at a given parish or institution could make up for and disguise these shortcomings. Today, limited energy and regular absenteeism are not so easily disguised or replaced. Bishops and personnel boards find themselves giving full and total pastoral responsibilities to men who could serve well and happily only in carefully limited capacities.

With regard to clouded personal future, for many, the declining number of active priests effectively dims any hopes for gentler years ahead and graceful retirement. Priests foresee themselves presiding at additional liturgies, responsible for more parishes and missions, and embroiled in added tensions over the consolidation and closure of parishes.

Despite clear church teaching, it is recognized that a source of discouragement for some priests is that some solutions to the clergy shortage are precluded from discussion and that not all pastoral solutions and options can be explored. Discouragement comes from the acute awareness of priests that some avenues of relief are not to be considered or discussed. Those most commonly referred to are ordination of married men, effective use of laicized priests, and expanded roles for women in ministry

In addition, the decline in active priests continues to stem not only from retirement and death, but also from resignation from the active ministry. Whether done quietly or with public repudiation of the church's discipline, these continuing resignations cause priests evident pain.

3. *Loneliness* is often mentioned by priests as a cause for anxiety and pain. Loneliness, the committee notes, is a common experience in all walks of life and a societal problem that has been particularly noted in the American male. However, the frequency with which the subject of loneliness is brought up by priests suggests that the fairly common observation that 'male' loneliness is part of the human condition and is equally true of married men is neither accurate nor helpful. The priest's need for intimacy, coupled with the distance sometimes created by the role of priest and the integrity demanded between the priest's feelings and public life, need greater attention.

4. Issues surrounding *sexuality* in culture and in the church today introduce other tensions. These issues touch on both personal and interpersonal levels of sexuality in terms of psychosexual development, personal integration of sexuality as a celibate, and changing understandings of sexuality and sexual orientation. There

are also stressors relating to the "politics of sexuality," which include issues surrounding feminism, married clergy, optional celibacy, and the role and place of homosexual men in ministry. The committee notes that generally every study or commentary done on the priesthood and shortage of vocations mentions sexuality (and specifically mandatory celibacy) as a major reason for (a) leaving the priesthood, (b) for shortage of vocations, and (c) for loneliness and personal unhappiness of those who stay.

5. *Differing perceived ecclesiologies* seems to be a source of demoralization that has grown steadily in recent years. The problem of polarization was addressed in a document entitled "The Priest and Stress":

> The priestly profession is one that must work within an ecclesial community that is polarized. Sometimes vastly differing notions of faith, ecclesiology, law, and ministry are to be found within the same rectory. This is a cause of tension, especially when individuals must not only work together but share common living arrangement. Polarization within dioceses and parishes can paralyze leadership, making it difficult, if not impossible, for a bishop or priest to obtain the consensus he needs to lead his people. Such polarization within communities, whose purpose for existing is deep unity of faith, can produce much frustration for priestly leaders. When a mentality of self-righteousness on either end of the theological spectrum exists, a debilitating wear on the person whose responsibility it is to try and forge some common understanding results. Sustained opposition from the people he serves, or other pastors or co-workers, will inevitably take its toll on any priest.

6. Priests feel demoralized from a *lack of affirmation*. On the one hand, the familiar clerical systems of recognition are largely ineffective

or inappropriate. Nomination to honorary titles and appointment to coveted parishes have disappeared as challenge, incentive, or reward. On the other hand, society and the media rarely deal with clergy or the church in affirming or even kindly fashion. Scandals among priests and other clergy persons take their toll. The church itself is perceived as an uncaring, legalistic institution.

The committee goes on to suggest that this profile paints a picture of the American priesthood as an institution in a "mid-life crisis." Priests fear that their youthful dreams and hopes will never be achieved; that the vision that they had seems to be slipping away or is now unimportant; that there is no possibility of the recognition or rewards once dreamed of. Priests feel that they have little control over their lives or futures, be it in terms of their lives and futures, be it in terms of ministry, assignment, policy development, or church direction.

So what is the experience of resignation from active ministry like for priests?

Meet John, Louis, and Mike.

John

Abstract

John resigned from active ministry at forty-six years of age. A convert to Catholicism, he entered seminary and later became a priest with little foreknowledge of priestly life and ministry. Exercising his priesthood principally in Europe and Canada, John suggests that inadequate psychosocial input in formation (pre-ordination) and lack of meaningful social support in ministry (post-ordination) were primary factors in his adherence to an external role to the detriment of an expanded personal consciousness including an acknowledgment of inner needs and dynamics.

Reflections on his own life experiences invite discussion on priestly formation and maintenance of healthy men pre- and post-ordination.

Orientation

My name is John. I am presently forty-eight years old. I entered the seminary in 1975 at twenty-five years of age. I was ordained at thirty-two years of age, and I resigned active ministry at forty-six years of age. I exercised most of my priesthood in Europe and Canada. I worked in parochial ministry, doing extensive administrative work in both urban and rural areas.

I am the oldest of four children. I have one brother and two sisters. I became a priest because of a desire to please God. I figured if becoming a priest was God's will, then I should do it. Having lived a difficult life before entering the seminary, I guess I wanted to secure a spiritual path. In part, I became a priest for the security that priesthood offered.

My Seminary Experience

My experience of formation in seminary was generally positive. I liked the studies, especially philosophy and theology. I was, however, sort of naive. Many other men in the seminary who had some sort of life experience ended up leaving. But me, well, I sort of accepted everything that was presented at face value. While the studies were interesting and the environment conducive to prayer, I felt that, as a group, we were treated as little kids. So I acted like a kid by leaving myself in the hands of other people, to whom I gave full responsibility for my life's direction. My formators determined what was or was not of importance to me.

There were enough positive experiences for me to stick with the formation experience, although there was something about the role of being a seminarian that I didn't like. Yes, I enjoyed teaching catechism to the children. There was plenty of time structured in for prayer. But I had a lot of mixed fears.

All during my seminary days, I was always hoping that someone would discover that I didn't belong there and send me away. As I said, I turned the responsibility of my life over to other people. I'm not saying that I was told to do this. The fact is, I didn't know what I felt and even less how to vocalize what was going inside me.

At the same time, I wanted to get married and have a family. So on retreats, I spoke with counselors and spiritual directors about this. They would say that I was being side-tracked by temptation. *Avanti* is the word in Italian. Just keep going…and I did. No one told me I should leave, and so I stayed.

Complicating action (sequence of events)

Ordination

Priesthood was a mixed blessing. Regarding my ministerial duties, I enjoyed working with people and preaching the most. I became very confident with the externals of my role. On the inside, however, I was dying. Sometime within the first three years of ministry, I told a friend of mine that I felt as if I were dying of a mortal disease. I just didn't fit in somehow, as if I were torn in two

This was a continuation of my seminary experience. I didn't allow myself to voice my suspicion that I shouldn't be there. I thought that if I just left everything in God's hands and closed my eyes to what was stirring inside me, then God would take care of things, so to speak. I never really voiced what I was feeling to other people. Even though I felt there was something wrong, I couldn't understand what "it" was.

I experienced a lack of support from other priests. In Italy, I was the new kid on the block. The other fathers were all thirty and forty years older than I. It didn't seem they had much of a life outside of the television. I don't think they liked Canadians that much, so I had little rapport with the other men in our community. I felt lonely and, at times, misunderstood. I'll give you an example.

They told me that I was going to say the twelve o'clock noon mass. Of all the masses celebrated, it was the least attended. When the pastor preached, he would go on and on for thirty or forty minutes, being vague and abstract. On the contrary, my homilies were always under ten minutes. Then the youth group brought guitars to the mass. The result was that people really started coming in great numbers and the church became full. The other priests became jealous, accusing me of trying to make a parish within a parish.

Evaluation (Meaning Subject Ascribes to the Experience)

After sixteen years, I finally took a sabbatical and looked into myself. It was then that I had to come to terms with this longing that I felt. When I started the work of renewal, I acknowledged that I had never had a real desire for priesthood. There was never any deeper call that I knew of, nor did any proper discernment of vocation prior to or after ordination take place. Yes, I always liked the work, preaching and working with the people. I didn't like the role of the priest in terms of the uncertain parameters. In retrospect, I understand now that I always thought that if I could go home from work after a certain time, it would have made a difference. I lived where I worked. I realize that I was always trying to make a family out of the place where I lived and worked. Once I left, I realized that I could never create a real family with those to whom I ministered or with those with whom I lived.

In the latter case, it seemed that everybody was workaholic. Sure, they were courteous and helpful, and that's about it. But it was never going to be any more than that.

There was never any one experience in my formation after ordination of which I would say, "This is the last straw." Sure, I can think of things that made me angry, but prior to any of these things, I recognized that I did not belong.

Resolution

Ultimately, I resigned from priesthood in an effort to be more honest to myself. I never desired priesthood, never chose it, and to go back would be a lie to myself and others. Now, if I felt some kind of interior call or attraction, I would certainly give it a try. But I never felt that. So I frame my leaving in very positive terms. I took the responsibility for my own life rather than just doing stuff for other people.

Now, again, I mentioned that I had been asking for a sabbatical for about eight years. I might say that, had I gotten my sabbatical eight years before, when I first started asking for it, maybe things would have turned out differently. Maybe I would have assimilated or internalized the values of priesthood. But my experience was that my community pretty well sucked everything out of me and then asked for more. And that made me angry.

In discerning my resignation, I had talked to my provincial for about five hours. He wouldn't say anything. He just kept saying, "Tell me more, tell me more." At the end of all of that, he didn't affirm anything, nor did he reflect back anything to me or acknowledge anything he heard. At the end of all that I shared, he said, "You're hurting many other people by doing this. We need you. You work well, and we want you back to work because there's a lot of work to do."

Here's a story that illustrates their deaf attitude toward me.

I was finishing up my last parochial assignment to take up duties as rector of the seminary. I was tired and requested a sabbatical prior to undertaking this new work. They said, "As rector of the seminary, you will have a different kind of a life. It will be more quiet and more centered around the prayer life. It will be like a sabbatical."

"'Like a sabbatical?'" I thought.

I was leaving a big job, and I now was going to a big job. So I reiterated that I needed a sabbatical. Finally, they said "Well, you come to New York, and we'll discuss this."

Now, you have to understand that this was January, and I'd not taken a day off since the fall. So, about two days before I was about to leave, they phoned me.

"When are you leaving?"

"I'm leaving in two days," I said. "I plan to go home for one week, and then I'm driving down to the seminary."

"You can't do that," said my provincial. "We have meetings starting in two days' time. You have to be here."

"I'm sorry," I said. "But I can't leave here today and start there the day after tomorrow. I'm tired," adding "you know all this is a big emotional drain on me."

But my provincial insisted.

"You're the new superior, and we can't have these meetings without you. You must be here."

"If this were so important," I said, "why didn't somebody tell me this before now?"

Finally, I said, "I'll think about it."

I put my thoughts on paper in a letter and sent it to him. I emphasized that it was not that I didn't want to attend, but that I just couldn't.

After receiving the letter, my provincial phoned me. He must have read his chosen response in a book somewhere, for he said, "I understand your needs," but concluded, "You have to be here. We need you."

Once again, I said, "I'll think about it."

"Well," I reasoned, "if I go straight to the seminary like he wants, then I can get all these meetings out of the way and then I can go home for vacation for a couple of weeks."

So I went.

Well, when I got to the seminary, it was one thing after another, and I could never leave. I was really sick and burned out at that point. I concluded that they just didn't consider my needs. They squeezed whatever they could get out of me, and then they asked for more.

There was a provincial and a couple of other people who had read in a book how it's supposed to be. That's it. It's black and white. So they were terribly angry. Like that's it, I'm going to hell, whatever. Then there were those who tried to understand where I was coming from, and, you know, it might have been painful for them. But they tried to give good support and tried to understand and accept whatever I chose.

My transition to a new role identity has been good. I'm part of a men's group that's been a good support to me. Um, I think the six-month sabbatical I had was part of the transition in that I discovered what was going on and to a certain extent began to work that out over the course of time. I have had a girlfriend now for two months. I think that's working out very well. But for a year and a half in transition before now, I was very happy just on my own. I've not been longing for or looking for anybody. If it happened, fine. If it didn't happen, fine. I was happy. I'd go out dancing and just have a good time with friends. So I never really longed much for anybody or anything.

My job for about the first year was very abusive. My boss was a real asshole. Evil. He eventually got fired, and then I took over his job for a couple of months. They hired a new director, who is wonderful. It's still a job where I get $32,000 per year, plus good health benefits. So it's still not sort of corporate-level stuff, but it's not bad. I have enough money to do everything that's necessary. I don't live luxuriously, but I'm not looking for that.

Reactions and Social Support for the Decision to Role Exit

Reactions to my decision to leave were mixed. My provincial and a couple men read in a book that once a priest, always a priest. That's it. It's black and white. So they were terribly angry when I decided to leave. Like "That's it, you're going to hell."

I don't have much contact with my former congregation now that I've resigned. If they were too busy before to have a relationship, imagine now. At present, I think they feel a little uncomfortable with me. They don't know what to say, and so now it doesn't work out very well. And then there are some of them that feel I've taken off on the family, and so I've betrayed them and their trust.

Coda: Present Self Perspective

While I miss the preaching and some of the work with the people, I feel for the first time in my life that there's no pot on the back burner. I do have some issues that have arisen recently for the first time in my life. This girlfriend and how we are handling things create some difficulty. But, now I'm a human being and feel very much at peace.

I don't have too many regrets about the priesthood. One of the things that I would have done differently is that I would have asked for a dispensation right away. There are many things in life that you can't see at the time. But for me, I see that every step has been necessary. If I was going to have a family or a job, it would have been better to have started when I was twenty. As far as my young adult life, I wish I had been more outspoken about my own feelings and needs early on. I wish I could have discerned and voiced them. But that was a weakness on my part. Now I see it as necessary to follow healthy truth and let whatever happens happen. I guess it's these sort of interior things that I would have done differently, and the consequences would have fallen a different way.

I really feel that prospective priests should be in groups like those in which I participate. Sexaholics Anonymous (SA) is for people with behavioral problems where sexuality is concerned. Codependency Anonymous (CODA) is for people with relationship styles that get them in trouble. Sex and Love Addicts Anonymous (SLAA) is the one that helps people get in touch with the whole person: emotion, sex, love, and the relational aspects of the human endeavor. So I think knowledge about and participation in such groups can be helpful. I went to CODA for a while, but that felt very superficial.

What I've learned is that I must not live a role to the point that I'm denying what's going on inside of me in order to live up to that role. I can no longer think that all I have to do is pray harder and work harder. If there's something wrong, then there's something wrong, and I need to look at it. Pain is a sign of something. I can't just pat myself on the back and think I'm a martyr when I'm in pain. That might be a sign that something's not right and I've got to attend to it.

As far as advice to persons in authority regarding priesthood and heathy living, I wouldn't begin with the Pope. I'm guessing he knows pretty well what the score is. It's the provincial—well, at least my provincial.

From my perspective, the Pope has been trying to get the bishops and provincials to do some of the things I've said, such as ongoing formation. If other bishops and provincials are like mine, they must put their books and studies aside and get their feet on the ground and truly listen in an attempt to understand where their supervisees are coming from. Provincials should not let their own duties and cares obstruct their hearing of what those for whom they are responsible are saying.

I recall indirectly sharing my feelings of stress or overwork with my provincial on the occasion of some big meeting we were attending together in New York. I was very candid, almost just talking to myself. I wasn't angry.

He responded by saying, "Well, I have so many things to do, including this upcoming talk to the postulants!"

My reply to him was, "Look, you may have your work to do, and your difficulties, and everything, but don't take away what my experience is." I felt that he lacked compassion and empathy. I mean, as provincial, you've got be able to get into the skin of other people. But again, that experience may not be generalizable to all provincials and bishops.

In conclusion, my leaving was difficult. I didn't feel I was divorcing a family where there had been enormous problems. It wasn't like I was getting rid of something that I couldn't get along in some adversarial way with and anger and hate and all such attendant emotions. Rather, my decision was proactive and, I feel, positive. I discovered something going on inside me that said, "You shouldn't be here...you should be somewhere else."

Yet my experience as a priest has been mainly positive, and I've been, generally, very happy. It might have been more positive if I'd been of single heart. But I was of divided heart. I sometimes wonder if, in a certain sense, I've never given priesthood a fair shake because I was divided all these years. I ask myself, how could I have discerned positively? To discern right, one must have attained a certain degree of peace and security. But from my present perspective, I never have felt called. Otherwise, I might give it another try and could probably do it a lot better.

So priesthood never became something that I wanted and felt comfortable with. If I had had more guidance, more ongoing formation, more aids to discernment, and more mentors who were closer in age to us in formation, things might have been different. When we went to our parish assignments as newly-ordained priests, we were young guys attempting to communicate with old pastors. I didn't grow up as a Catholic, so I never saw what a priest was supposed to do. I had to learn it on my own. So if I had had ongoing formation and contact with an empathetic, experienced mentor prior to and after ordination, that might have changed things.
Louis

Abstract

Louis resigned from active ministry at forty years of age after sixteen years as a priest. After his seminary formation and subsequent ordination to priesthood, he was assigned to teach in a diocesan seminary in Ireland. Finding that this work lacked sufficient challenge and investment of self, he volunteered for a mission assignment in Chile. After fourteen years, he came to terms with the two issues that were most significant in his determination to transition from active ministry: celibacy and Church teaching, especially as these relate to the document *Humane Vitae.*

Orientation

My name is Louis. When I was eighteen, I entered the seminary to begin my studies to become a Roman Catholic priest. I was ordained at twenty-four years of age. My first assignment was to teach English, history, and religion in high school, which I did for three years. My life was comfortable as a priest from the start. Most of my basic needs were well met. Economically, I was well off.

From an early age, I wanted to become a priest. I was influenced in this direction by the example of priests that I knew as a boy. At the same time, our grammar school teacher had me selling magazines dealing with the Church's missionary efforts in Africa. I also had an uncle that was a priest. In essence, I envisioned myself as bringing the Word of God to people in foreign lands. After three years as a high school teacher, Pope John asked that 10 percent of the clergy go to foreign missions. So at about age twenty-seven, I felt the need to make the most of my talents as well as gets to know a little more of the world. The opportunity to go to mission in Chile presented itself. I took it.

I was very happy in my mission assignment. After a couple of initial living changes, I was assigned to a small parish community in the Chilean countryside. I lived with another priest four years older than myself.

Complicating Action (Sequence of Events)

I met Maria.

While I had been attracted to other women, I never expressed this to any of them. With Maria, seven years went by before I expressed having any feeling for her. There were several other things that happened that made me acknowledge my feelings. Pope Paul's declaration against the use of artificial contraception, <u>Humanae Vitae</u>, was promulgated. This document was presented as infallible, and I couldn't accept this. As the oldest of eight children myself, I knew that the more kids parents have, the bigger their problems are. How often I'd put my hands in my pocket and given someone with a sick child the last few pesos I had. It seemed that infallibility was more important than the reality of a growing world population and so on. So my faith in the church from the perspective of the Magisterium was rattled at that stage.

During this time, I became distanced from Eucharist (Mass). My superiors expressed concern for me. They appreciated the work that I was doing, but at the same time offered other working options and environments. I never talked to them about Maria.

For more than ten years, I struggled with the meaning of my feelings towards Maria. Intermittently, we would go to the capital, Santiago, to do work for the Cooperative. Maria and I would meet in the city. While in the process of trying to decide whether to stay in ministry or to leave, the question of children came up. That was the moment of truth for me, and I decided I could straddle the fence no longer. It was time to go.

The first thing I had to do was find a job. My congregation gave me some initial financial assistance. My first job was teaching kids metalwork. Then I got a job at the Catholic University teaching English as a second language.

We really wanted to stay in South America, but with the money devaluating and our first child on the way, we just couldn't see it. My brother in New York invited me to come to the United States. And so we went.

I had spoken with my parents about the possibility of my leaving the priesthood. Dad was better with this idea than Mom. I went home alone, and my parents both were very good to me. Dad wanted me to bring my wife home and live there. He suggested that I'd run the farm with him again. But I felt it would have been an impossible situation with my mom and my wife together. So I never brought her home with me, and they never met Maria.

Coda: Evaluation (Meaning Subject Ascribes to the Experience)

I resigned from priesthood basically because I needed a woman. I'm happy that I left and that I'm not suffering like I was. I thank God for this.

In retrospect, I think I needed more freedom, including being able to choose someone to love. That was the problem that started from the time I was ordained. Perhaps if celibacy were an option, problems with priests, highlighted in the media, would be less prevalent.

I would return to ministry today if I had liberty. By this, I mean to be able to see that revelation happens over time. It's not magic and "given." And there are still more things to hammer out. So you just can't go to "the Word of God" or the Magisterium and shut everybody up. The Bible reflects an experience that was hammered out over six or seven hundred years with all kinds of rows and fights over what books should be in and what books shouldn't be in and so on

Such thinking scares people and threatens their comfort zones. They don't want to have to think too much or have their faith shaken. So I'd like to be a priest again, but only if I could live and teach a kind of Liberation Theology.

At sixty-five, I am happy with my life. I've enjoyed raising my children and teaching Spanish poetry and literature. I suppose that, in this way, I am still a priest. But now I see that being a good human is more important than being a priest. As God's creature, wearing uniforms or belonging to a special group is less important to me now.
Mike

Abstract

Mike began his seminary training upon completion of high school. He was ordained at twenty-six years of age and resigned at age thirty-five. He admits having difficulty with celibacy from the time he began his seminary career, but found little helpful direction from those overseeing his formation process. His disaffection from the clerical role was incremental. He assumed that somehow his difficulties with celibacy would be resolved, and that he would remain committed to his priestly role and identity. He found little comfort or support from the "fraternity of priests." His peers knew of his apparent difficulties with celibacy and commented about this to one another, but not to Mike himself. Mike's bishop's lack of appreciation of, and support for, Mike's effort to achieve congruency between his outward role and inward personal developmental processes was common to most of those interviewed.

Abstract

Orientation (Time, Place, Situation)

My name is Mike.

Upon completing high school, I entered the seminary. I was eighteen at the time. Throughout Catholic grammar school and high school, I thought about becoming a priest, but never seriously. I admired the priests and nuns that I saw on a regular basis. Our parents encouraged us kids to consider the priesthood and religious life, although I don't recall anyone coming to me in high school and saying, "You ought to become a priest."

When I was a high school senior, I applied to the University of Houston. I desired to major in science. I remember one high school classmate saying that he was going into the seminary. So I asked for an application too. Today, this man is a geologist, and I became a priest. As priesthood was always in the back of my mind, I decided to follow my parents' advice and give it a try.

Seminary

In seminary graduate school (first theology), I recognized I had a problem with celibacy. At that time, I thought about taking a leave of absence and exploring this issue. I pursued the topic with my spiritual director, who suggested that I drop the issue, as it wasn't that important. As it turned out, he himself left to marry. Year to year, the celibacy issue kept coming back. I knew that I had not really come to grips with it. I had never had a one-on-one relationship with a woman and so never needed to think about getting married. I drifted.

In the seminary, we didn't address the sexual self. I brought this up to my spiritual director, but now recognize he had issues of his own. I don't know if he was uncomfortable in pursuing the topic of celibacy. Just looking back, I think it just got overlooked. I knew a lot of friends were really struggling, and I thought the fact that I wasn't really struggling was a blessing. I took it as a sign. While it never became a decisive issue during my formation, I knew in the back of my mind it was something I hadn't really tackled. I guess I knew that once I became ordained, down the road, I was going to deal with it. Celibacy was something that I knew I would have to come to grips with down the road.

Celibacy figured in from the start. I was a first-class nerd in high school. I really had no involvement with girls. I went on a few double dates, but not any one-on-one relationships. So it came to my mind, well, since I don't have marriage in my future, I'll go with the fact that I'm celibate right now and go with it.

Ironically, the lady I ended up marrying, Gwen, was one of the first people I met in my new assignment. So celibacy became an issue within the first month of ordination. In a sense, looking back on the priesthood experience, I never knew priesthood without having to deal with the celibacy issue. I knew that celibacy was a challenge, and I believed that somehow my relationship with Gwen was going to come to an end. I felt very strongly about the commitment I had made. I knew a lot of people who had left the ministry, and somehow, I did not see myself in their company.

Now, I had a friend that was in ministry. He was in a relationship with a woman. The way he dealt with it was that he would remain in the ministry and that she would just be…there. And after a period of time, I realized that there was something wrong with this. With Gwen and me, this would not be an option.

I enjoyed the priesthood. It was sacred. I felt that I was doing something that was really special. I saw those to whom I ministered as wanting to be closer to God and God-like. This did something for me.

While I like the ministry, I didn't enjoy rectory living. In a sense, you were thrown in with other men in a virtual marriage that you didn't want to be in. At least, I didn't want to be in. I noticed this when I was a deacon.

Complicating Action: Sequence of Events

My "first doubts" came real quick. It was the celibacy issue.

Gwen was active in the parish: CYO, different committees. We did a lot of work together. About a year after ordination, it became obvious that Gwen and I were having feelings for each other. The way I dealt with that was that I said to myself, "I won't leave." While it was difficult, I was able to admit to Gwen that I loved her.

An official in the diocese came to me in an informal way, stating that he had heard that I was seeing "so and so" from some priests at a party. He was letting me know that my brother priests knew. He suggested that I was the object of ridicule; that other priests were talking about me. No concrete help or suggestions were offered. In retrospect, it may have been a good thing. I was rationalizing. I was having this relationship, figuring that no one knew, or if they did know, no one really cared. So I was forced to confront my situation—"shit or get off the pot." At that point, I was thinking about getting some counseling to help me pursue the idea of a decision to stay in or to leave ministry.

Once I began counseling, I continued in therapy for a couple of years. Since our relationship was getting serious, and I hadn't talked to anybody about it, I was able to get things off my chest. Eventually, she went to counseling too. So there was no one last straw. Everything just seemed to come together.

Evaluation and Resolution

The biggest issue for me was, should I stay in priesthood or should I leave. I figured the rest would take care of itself. I didn't think of alternative employment. I knew that I could survive about a year with what I had saved. So finally, I made the decision to leave the priesthood.

But leaving priesthood was unthinkable. From the beginning, I envisioned myself as someone who would stay with it. It was all very traumatic.

The worst part was telling my parents. I had never discussed this with them before. They were aware of Gwen, but they weren't aware of the level of our involvement. Dad was more aware than Mom. She figured that we were friends in the platonic sense. It was so hard for me to bring it up that I just wrote them a letter. Then, on the phone, I broke down. In my family, divorce was unheard of. Once you made a commitment, you stuck with it.

Talking to the bishop was equally difficult. As with my parents, I wrote to my bishop asking him for a leave of absence. He thought that taking me from the rectory/parish situation and putting me in hospital ministry would help. So I was assigned to the hospital corps. I decided I would transition from ministry altogether. So I called and set up an appointment.

My sense was that he had not a clue about what I was talking about. For him, the only decision was either "you're in or you're out," and the only choice was for me to be in. He suggested I go to the Diocese of _____ and not tell anyone, especially not Gwen, where I was going. They needed the help up there, and I could be stashed away from the source of my temptation. I felt unsettled. While I knew it was there all along, he forced the issue. He offered no help other than this.

I felt traumatized. I've heard of women who have been raped wanting to take a shower after the experience. Well, I had this same feeling after meeting with the bishop. After leaving his office, I wanted to take a shower.

As for my brother priests, I never mentioned my situation to any of them. I didn't feel close to many of them. Those whom I was close to were from other dioceses.

My first employment on leaving ministry was temporary work cleaning commodes. I did this for several weeks. I realized that I knew each commode by name and could recognize each blemish in each commode. I realized, "Whoa, it's time to get out of this." So during the earliest days of my transition, I was looking for something else. I belonged to CORPUS and received a publication called *Woerk*. *Woerk* was a newsletter for priests in transition and looking for work.

Here I saw something about probation. It made me look into the phone book for government listings, where I found the probation department. I called and told somebody about myself. He invited me in for an initial interview. I was hired during that first contact. I've been there since.

Before I married, I applied to be laicized. It wasn't granted until I was out for ten years. I've heard from others that after ten years, a laicization is automatically given. I guess there's something magical with the church and a ten-year mark. Perhaps at this point, it is assumed that you're not going to come back or that you've suffered enough, or whatever. I don't know. So after ten years, we went to the local pastor at our hometown parish, and we had our marriage blessed.

Coda

I had a dream once that my becoming a priest was just a dream. In my dream, I felt extremely relieved that I hadn't taken that step to become a priest. But then I awoke.

It would have made things a lot easier if I had not been ordained when I was. But then it gets into other things. For example, I would have never met Gwen, and so on. I don't think there was anything anybody could have said or done that would have prevented my resignation. After I was ordained, I heard comments by some people that I shouldn't have been ordained. They suggested that I should have pursued the celibacy issue more. But this was never told me before. Had someone confronted me beforehand, it would have been a favor to me. But from where I presently sit, I don't think I would have done anything differently.

I don't fault anybody for what I've done. If there's any fault, it's with me. I just feel for the guys who are going through this. I know what a struggle it is. I just hope they have someone they can confide in.

Summary

The popular image (in the Catholic world) of the ex-priest as immature and disgruntled, radical, overly concerned with fulfilling his own needs and so reneging on his vows or promises, fails against the complex portrait that emerges in this brief profiling of three ex-clerics. What has been shown in these stories is that the category of ex-priest includes men who began their preparation for ministry in adolescence and early adulthood, assumed their ministry as ordained priests with sincerity and an earnest intent towards a lifetime commitment, and were surprised by their inability to maintain an authentic and congruent commitment to priesthood through their middle years.

These ex-priests hold their priesthood in high regard, reflecting with gratitude on their past exercise of ministry. Those profiled reliably reflect the major characteristics of the larger sample of inactive priests. If, as a group, ex-priests are not very different from priests who continue in ministry, then there may be reason to suspect that exit may have something to do with structural problems in the Catholic Church itself rather than background factors which predispose individual priests to exit.

I exercised my own priestly ministry with the courageous people of Central America in the 1980s. It was a time of civil war. On occasion, I collected the remains of bound and murdered people, left to bake amidst trash strewn about in the hot tropical sun. President Ronald Reagan drew the line against communism in the Western Hemisphere in El Salvador. By virtue of training and arming the Salvadoran military, the U.S. pitted itself against the Catholic Church in this tiny nation. The Diocese of San Salvador based its pastoral plan on the "preferential option for the poor." Catholics suddenly found themselves described as terrorists, subversives, Communists.

Oscar Romero, bishop of San Salvador, is a premier model for the individuation process. He did not back away from speaking the truth, whether in personal or social matters. By listening to his pastoral agents as well as his people, he came to see the connection between militarism and poverty and to address this with courage. "Before an order to kill that a man may give," Romero told the soldiers who had surrounded the Cathedral on March 23, 1980, "the law of God must prevail that says: 'Thou shall not kill.'" Not a sound could be heard in that vacuous, concrete structure on that fateful morning. "No soldier," Romero declared, "is obliged to obey an order against the law of God."

His invitation to disobedience based on a Gospel mandate sealed his fate. Thirty hours later, Bishop Oscar Romero lay in a pool of blood, murdered while celebrating the Eucharist.

I too am charged to speak the truth as best as I can. And so are you.

ABOUT THE AUTHOR

William Schmidt is the author of <u>Standing Tall: Doing Justice in Time of War</u>. He holds a Ph.D. from the University of Houston and his Master of Divinity from Immaculate Conception Seminary in Huntington, New York. He is a licensed professional counselor, social worker and psychotherapist. He is married to Ana Beatriz and they have three children: Ana Leticia, John Thomas and Bill.

LaVergne, TN USA
02 November 2009
162829LV00004B/1/P